Awaken the Will to Love

A Guide to Personal and Collective Transformation
Through Meditation and Psychosynthesis

Uta Gabbay

Awaken the Will to Love
A Guide to Personal and Collective Transformation through Meditation and Psychosynthesis

Copyright @2018 Uta Gabbay

Uta Gabbay has asserted her right to be identified as the author of this book. All rights reserved, including the right to reproduce or transmit this book, or portions thereof, in any form, except in the form of brief quotations.

Cover design by Alon Gabbay
Cover image by Filippo Bassano
Edited by Spencer Borup

www.hechal.org

Dedicated with joy and gratitude to my coworkers, past and present, in the Hechal Centre for Universal Spirituality in Jerusalem.

I would like to express my gratitude to our many precious coworkers around the world, and especially to our friends from the Community of Living Ethics (www.comunitadieticavivente.org) in Italy for their sustained support and cooperation.

Thank you also to my tree friends in the Italian and German forests for holding the space for me during my long hours of walking and pondering and writing in their shade.

Gratitude to Orit Loyter for our deep contemplations throughout the years and her sharp-minded accompaniment of my writing process.

Table of Contents

Introduction 7
The Tools 11
  PSYCHOSYNTHESIS 11
  MEDITATION 13
  How to Use This Book 17
Personal Transformation 22
  Sense of Self 22
  The Physical Body 23
  The Emotions 24
  The Mind 28
  The Personality 32
  The Power to Disidentify 35
  The Inner Director 37
  Looking Inwards – Self-Observation 41
  Looking Upwards – The Soul 43
  Looking Outwards – Ready to Expand 46
  Relationship 47
  White Magic 49
  Subtle Patterns 51
The Group as a Transformation Tool 55
  A Word about Groups 55
  The Group Field 58
  The Group Purpose 61
  The Group Focaliser 63
  Group Coherence through the Seven Rays 66
  The Group as an Instrument for the Common Good 69
Collective Transformation 72
  About Collective and National Fields 72

Hechal's First Experience with a Collective Field 73
Assagioli's Psychosynthesis of a Nation... 76
How to Work with a National Field 78
The Group of Best Citizens.. 79
Towards a Scientific Attitude 83
Looking Inwards – Observing the National Personality................. 86
The Physical Field of a Nation... 86
The Emotional Field of a Nation 87
The Mental Field of a Nation... 88
Looking Upwards – Invoking the National Soul 92
Looking Outwards – Formulating a Vision for the Nation........... 94
Implementing the Vision.. 95

Introduction

A great planetary transformation is under way as our old world is falling apart.

This is not an easy time for anyone on this planet, and yet it is also a great opportunity for each of us. It forces us to fall back on our own resources, on the power of our own hearts and minds. We have the choice to either radically transform and upgrade ourselves and become agents of change, or be passively and cluelessly swept along.

This book is for people who want to seize the day, for themselves and for our world. It provides a step-by-step guide to shape up for planetary transformation, on three levels: in our personal lives, as members of groups, and as participants in the collective.

It is the fruit of my over-twenty-years of experience as spiritual psychotherapist and meditation teacher in Jerusalem. Built on the model of Psychosynthesis in combination with the technique of meditation, it provides a new way to understand the human being – with all our patterns and powers – and a clear and logical sequence of procedure to manage the patterns and awaken the powers into much higher functioning.

This method is based on a simple fact: 'Energy follows thought.'[1] This means that wherever we focus our attention is where action will take place. There, something will happen. It boils down to the fact that by learning to direct our inner life we can direct our outer reality. Psychosynthesis explains the inner mechanism and meditation supplies the 'technology' to effectively run it.

The first part of the book provides a step-by-step program of personal transformation. Each step is accompanied by meditative

---

[1] 'Energy follows thought' is one of the key premises on which esoteric philosophy is built. It was first coined by Alice Bailey.

exercises, which are potent tools of inner change, forged through years of work with many individuals and groups.

As we change and expand our consciousness, our own personal happiness cannot remain an isolated island. We cannot really be happy if our family is not happy as well. And our nation cannot really flourish if our neighbors do not flourish alongside us.

Together, we will begin to grasp the fact that, truly, all is related. Humanity struggles to shift from separation-consciousness to relation-consciousness. Relation-consciousness will then naturally bring about peace.

For me, that big word – 'peace' – translates into *coherence*, or *wholeness*, starting with each individual integrating their heart and mind and will into a harmoniously functioning whole. The Hebrew word *Shalom* – 'peace' – literally translates to *wholeness*. When many such islands of wholeness connect, they strengthen each other and build up towards a critical mass.

Thus, the agents of this planetary shift are awakened, empowered human beings, motivated towards the common good.

This process is taken to the next level when we learn to work as groups; groups, when functioning as coherent wholes, become magnets with a much greater transformative power and a much wider field of influence.

The later part of the book takes up the process of building such 'transformation groups' as catalysts for personal development and as potent instruments of service to the wider collective. Groups, when working together, can transform collectives.

The principles of transformation are the same for individuals, groups, and collectives.

So peace is a process with underlying laws and a logical sequence, in which each of us can and must participate. We cannot wait any longer for the right political leader to finally make it happen.

My passion to contribute to this peace pulled me out of my native Germany at an early age and planted me in Jerusalem for thirty-five years, during which time I founded the **Hechal Centre for Universal Spirituality**. *Hechal* means 'sacred space' in Hebrew. It started out as a school for meditation and took on additional layers over the years that followed. Beyond running meditation courses for the various populations in Jerusalem, our collegial team became a laboratory for the science of group work. This work has further evolved into an experiment of what some call 'spiritual activism': we employ our inner powers of heart, mind, and will in group formation and in cooperation with coworkers around the world, on behalf of the common good.

One such project is our work with the Jewish people, as I describe later in this book. I, coming from a German Christian background, have grappled with them during my long years in Jerusalem; our group work was a big help in understanding and clearing my own 'Jewish issues'. Now, walking the woods surrounding my childhood village in Germany, I sometimes come across one of the small Jewish cemeteries tucked away in the far corners of the forest. They are peaceful places today, embraced by majestic oaks and motherly beeches. Forest of beeches – 'Buchenwald' in German. So strange. I can feel the pain, the heaviness that was, between Germans and Jews. And I can feel the healing energy from the trees. In this healing energy I don't know if I walk here as a German or as a Jew. I walk here as a human, holding in my heart this relationship which is in the process of healing. I truly feel, after all these years, that my Jewish brothers and sisters are family. I am a part of them, as I am a part of the German people in this lifetime. I feel a relief, a gratefulness, a letting go.

This part of me, this relationship within me, has found peace.

We know that all we need lies within us. We have the power to create happiness for ourselves, and we have the power to co-create peace. The state of our world calls out to each of us to step up to it, to find that power within, to train and use it.

This book provides a proven, safe, and efficient method for awakening our hearts and minds and wills and employing them for our own and for the common good – for our families, our groups, our nations, and our planet. Let us Awaken our Will to Love, to navigate through the present chaos and use it together to save our world.

The Tools

PSYCHOSYNTHESIS

Everyone has heard about meditation – but what of Psychosynthesis?

Here is how I encountered it:

Already as a teenager I felt the calling to inquire into the mystery of human nature, to somehow help run the complex business of Earth life more successfully. I left Germany at an early age on a quest for higher and more inclusive knowledge. I studied the mystics of all religions and spiritual teachings I could find. I realised that all beliefs expressed different aspects of the same universal wisdom. The theosophical stream appealed to me the most; it seemed to express this universality the most comprehensively. The teachings of Alice Bailey, Lucille Cedercrans, Agni Yoga, Anthroposophy, *A Course in Miracles*, and others became my spiritual home.

My travels brought me – through a magical journey of coincidences – to Jerusalem, where I knew I must stay without knowing why. I complemented my spiritual studies with an academic education, receiving a BA in Psychology of Education and Indian Studies from the Hebrew University in Jerusalem, and a degree in psychotherapy according to Carl Rogers, from Germany. I rounded out my therapeutic education with a number of alternative trainings of spiritual psychotherapy.

Out of all these teachings I developed my own blend of spiritual psychotherapy. After many years of practice, one day a colleague put two books into my hands: *Psychosynthesis* and *The Act of Will* by Roberto Assagioli.

Psychosynthesis can be briefly described as one of the founding stones of the Transpersonal Psychology movement in Europe, USA, and Australia. It is best known as a 'psychology with a soul' – or, to explain it another way, a spiritual psychotherapy – it brings together modern psychology, the wisdom of spiritual traditions, and the practice of introspection and meditation.

Much of its process is a comprehensive self-inquiry, which addresses not only the psychological contents but also the inner structure of the human being itself – our physical, emotional, and mental instruments. In order to build a healthy and strong personality, each of these instruments needs to be developed and fine-tuned and later integrated into one whole. In the process of integration, a unifying inner centre is established – which is called by Assagioli and in Hechal the 'conscious self'.

On the basis of such an integrated personality, a wider synthesis is then pursued – that between the personal self and the trans-personal self, or in other words, between the personality and the soul.

The more these two distinct centres of consciousness are brought into resonance and later into fusion, the more a full self emerges – a spiritual-human being.

Psychosynthesis presents this psycho-spiritual development as a structured scientific process.

I immediately felt at home in this system. It seemed to grow out of my own world picture; it also had the same quality of the heart, the same loving and universal approach, which I endeavoured to provide for the people I worked with. I was pleased to discover that I was actually already using some of the exercises in the Psychosynthesis manual; still others were so familiar to me that I felt I could have written them myself. I surmised that Assagioli must surely come from the same spiritual background; however, since in those days there didn't exist an easy Google access to information, I didn't pursue this thought any further. I just adopted a few features into my therapeutic practice and laid the books aside.

Over the years, I increasingly recognised Assagioli's work as a practical synthesis of the same universal wisdom teachings I had pursued from early adulthood; moreover, he applied them, among others, to the same fields of service I had chosen. With each new phase in my work, I would quite unexpectedly be introduced to yet another part of Assagioli's work which corroborated mine – first when I built my meditation school, then years later in my group work, and finally again, years later, in my work with the wider collective.

Most surprising was my discovery that he held extensive work with the Jewish people, all of which completely corroborated my own.

Therefore, Assagioli will accompany us throughout the process of this book. Furthermore, because he has captured the sometimes complex concepts of the universal wisdom teachings in such brilliant simplicity, I have also adopted his terminology.

While the universal wisdom teachings are my conceptual framework, what turns them into a complete working method is the technique of meditation.

MEDITATION

In my counselling work I became aware of the limitations of verbal exchange. I realised that oftentimes a verbal interaction, even if therapeutic, doesn't touch more than the mind, cannot penetrate to the roots where the deep issues are met and where change must take place.

When a person closes his or her eyes and looks, feels, and senses inwards, something else happens: the rational mind no longer controls the situation. We seem to have access to more layers of our being: our unconscious part, our physical sensations, our emotions, and also to something higher – a higher wisdom. A whole new world opens up.

With this realization, I started to introduce more and more meditative exercises into my private practice.

The word 'meditation' comes from the Latin *meditare*, or 'to ponder the centre'. Simply put, it is introspection – looking inside oneself. It means to ask the question 'Who am I?' in ever deeper and deeper ways.

In this way, meditation is actually the most direct method to get to know oneself. It is an intensely personal and spiritual experience, a subjective approach to knowing oneself and, by extension, the world. It is a much fuller experience than merely thinking or talking can ever be.

My own spiritual training opened and guided me through this inner world and I wanted to help others achieve a safe and ordered access to it – access beyond what personal psychotherapy can do.

When I began teaching meditation, I gleaned from various wisdom teachings and from my psychotherapeutic practice what seemed practical as first steps for beginners.

I had always liked leading meditations – the magic of choosing the right sequence, the right words, and the right tone of voice to create a path for people to follow with closed eyes!

It began as a series of evening classes for my neighbours in my small village outside Jerusalem. When they asked me for a continuation of the studies, I built a structured weekly training program for a full academic year.

Meditative exercises bring up new ideas, discoveries about our inner world, and even new states of consciousness. They are difficult to grasp at first, much like dream memories. Beginner students often come out of a meditation with the sense that something important has happened to them, but they can't find words for it. So I developed a method, through targeted and meditatively probing questions, to help the students formulate their experiences. This process of 'form-ulation' is vital: it creates a graspable 'form' for the subtle, subjective experiences – those which happen in the right hemisphere of the brain – thereby bringing (connecting) them safely into the left hemisphere, where they can be conceptualized and stored, thus becoming accessible to our everyday consciousness.

The effort of each student to thus put into words their precious inner experiences added much value for the other participants, and it developed an atmosphere in these group meetings, which encouraged the students to go deeper in their meditations, to share experiences which felt weird or frightening or embarrassing.

As the students delved deeper into their inner waters, a need for a second foundational year course arose, which I called 'Sense of Self'. In this course, I covered in greater detail the various aspects of the personality and also began to build an alignment with the soul.

And here we came to a fork in the program. There were those students who wanted to go even deeper into understanding themselves, and there were those who were more interested in how to apply these inner tools to their outer lives. So I found myself developing two parallel new courses.

One is called 'The Seven Rays'. This is an advanced model for understanding and managing the dynamics within oneself, in a group, and in wider contexts. We will get to know it later on.

The other course I called 'White Magic'. This is the name that the universal wisdom teachings give to the skill of employing the spiritual will to create our life consciously and effectively.

Energy follows thought. We have met this basic premise already in the introduction. As soon as we realize that this is not only an interesting philosophical concept, but a reality, we start to pay attention to the tremendous power we have through the instrument of our mind. Experiencing this power in the act of creating our individual reality will sooner or later lead us to the recognition that we have a gift to give to our world. We start using the power of our thoughts and consecration of our hearts on behalf of our family, our community, our nation, and the whole planet.

Here, meditation can grow beyond being a tool for personal development; it can also be used as a service to others and to the world.

I have developed a technique, which I call 'Meditative Inquiry'. It grew out of a request from a group of psychologists with whom I did regular peer supervision. They wanted to learn to use meditation in their therapeutic work.

Meditative Inquiry is a process of reflection done from an aligned inner state. By learning to focus our mind in different and specific ways, we have a veritable flashlight which can be directed at any object of our choice, be it within our own self or outside of us. It can throw light on any and all issues. This skill was gradually developed into a course which I call 'Psychic Investigation'. It trains the practitioner's finer senses, or so-called 'extra-sensory perceptions', to be used on behalf of another person, and it can also be employed to explore and improve our participation in a wider collective, both of which we will later see.

When engaging in meditation as a group, it takes on an added dimension. Thirty years ago our small Full Moon meditation group was a very pioneering endeavour. Today, a growing number of people are waking up to the potential of group meditation as a service to humanity. Now, in most cities, there are Full Moon meditations. When harnessed and directed correctly, the power of a group can become a great instrument for addressing a world problem or supporting a cause for the common good. And when groups align with each other in global meditations, they create a grid of goodwill – a network of light, love, and spiritual power – contributing to the harmonizing of our planetary field. This is a new way to make ourselves useful in our world: 'spiritual activism' on the inter-group level.

In retrospect I see how the development of this meditation school I just described to you was not random, but, by responding to the growing needs and capabilities of my students, followed a logical sequence. In the following chapters, I will trace much of this sequence for you.

How to Use This Book

It is challenging to convey and replicate in a book the experience of physical meditation meetings. The presence of others who sharpen their mental focus and make available their loving hearts creates a high-quality atmosphere, a telepathic field in which higher-than-usual impressions and states of consciousness can be reached and registered.

In this book, we will employ a number of measures to approximate this ideal atmosphere. As I have just described, in my courses I teach mainly through meditative exercises or short texts to which the students listen with closed eyes.

The texts in this book are written in a similar meditative way. Since one cannot read with one's eyes closed, I suggest you read quite slowly instead, to take your time with each segment, perhaps even with each paragraph. Read meditatively. Pause often and think. Feel. Allow yourself to ponder and brood. This is so different from what we are used to doing in today's world where every second counts – but counts towards what? To where? It takes willpower to counteract our default of accelerating and projecting ourselves outwards into the world, to instead turn inwards, decelerating.

The texts are accompanied by meditative exercises which build one on the other. These exercises appear in the text in Italics for easier locating.

The key exercises, taken from my courses, are numbered in each segment, and are also available as audio files, using this link: www.hechal.org/awl-audios

To have an outer voice guide you through an exercise has various benefits; therefore, I strongly recommend using the audio files. You can go much deeper into the experience, since you don't need to worry about memorising the instructions or pacing the exercise. Also, the voice of an experienced meditation teacher can subtly carry you along over unfamiliar terrain.

Naturally I cannot include all the many exercises that go with each segment during my courses, but you will find mini-exercises – or pointers – here and there, which take only moments. They start with 'Take a moment', and that's what I recommend you do whenever you see this prompt. Take it as a signal to stop reading and take a moment to look inside yourself.

Taking the inner step to actually practice these exercises makes the difference between reading an interesting book and embarking on an experiential journey.

I recommend and wish for each reader that you make use of these exercises, and more than that, that you allow them to become the guiding thread through the inner process outlined in this book. They can lead you deeper than any text – if you allow them to.

These exercises can become precious work tools, especially with repeated use.

You may choose to work with an exercise several times before advancing to the next segment in this book. The deeper you let the experience penetrate, the wider you open the door to new insights and states of being.

I suggest you get a notebook to accompany you on this process. As I described earlier, the effort of formulating your experiences, especially after a meditative exercise, makes a huge difference to the benefit you will get from this process. Although we can sometimes lose something of the original experience while trying to confine it into word 'forms', even the most resistant students in my meditation school did after a while bring their notebooks to class, because the gain outweighs by far the loss. As described earlier, the process of formulating the delicate experience gives it substance, makes it part of your consciousness. You will be able to remember it, come back to it, build on it.

It is beneficial to create a suitable space for the practice of meditation – a safe and beautiful ambience as free as possible from any human and/or device intrusion. You may want to create your own atmosphere, through a candle perhaps, or a crystal or other meaningful and uplifting objects.

Three more points before we open the floor to the actual experience:

1. All of the meditative exercises contained in this book have been forged and fine-tuned over many years with a large number of students. They have become quite powerful tools. However, not every tool fits everyone. I want to encourage you to rely on your own inner sense of rightness. If an exercise doesn't feel right to you, don't do it. And if an aspect of an exercise – for instance, a symbol or a color – doesn't feel precise to you, please feel free to change it. After giving a chance to the exercise and seeing that something in it doesn't work for you, experiment with changing the different elements to suit your inner needs.

2. A point of warning about meditation and mind-altering substances:

Both give you a greater freedom from the habitual patterns and states of consciousness, as well as a heightened sense of awareness. Through meditation practise you are using your own inner muscles to stretch beyond your habit. Drugs do it for you without your own efforts, and by this they can actually weaken your subtle infrastructure – your willpower, the integrity of your feelings, the clarity of your judgement – while meditation builds and strengthens it. When you combine drugs and meditation, the opening of the perception can be enhanced beyond your intention, and if your infrastructure is weak, you can lose control and do damage to yourself.

I don't say that mind-altering or psycho-active substances are always a bad choice. Many ancient and current spiritual traditions have their sacred substances to help the practitioner on their path. When done in a ceremonial setting and with pure intention, they can be great enhancers of the spiritual journey. However, especially for the beginner, they can become a dangerous trap.

With my students I talked this through and made specific agreements which I could monitor, also pertaining to psychiatric medicines. Of course, I cannot do this for the reader of this book. So on this subject I just say: give this careful thought and decide wisely.

3. And lastly, in terms of physical posture during the meditative exercises, it is recommended to sit comfortably, with your spine relatively straight, so that the subtle energy can flow unimpeded and a sense of vertical alignment can develop. However, if you would like to experiment with lying down or with any other posture, I invite you to go ahead and explore what works for you.

The exercises in later chapters concerning the group and collective work are ideally done in a group context. They can still be done by an individual, through the use of the imagination, by following the exercises as if you are part of a group. A nice compromise for experimenting with these exercises would be to find a 'study buddy': to explore them together with a friend.

So let us start right away with the first meditation. This first exercise has the purpose of bringing you into the present moment, thereby clearing the mind and setting the stage for the new project you are about to begin.

You may consider doing this exercise at the beginning of each work session. Of course you can use it for other projects as well. Each time you do it, you strengthen your capacity to be fully in the present moment.

Basic Meditation – Be Here Now

*****

Close your eyes.

Take a few deep breaths into your belly. Feel your body. Help the body relax and be comfortable. Gradually now, let go of all that is related to the past and of all that is related to the future. Allow yourself to take a short break from everything, from all your memories and all your plans. Let go for just a little while of all responsibilities. Let your attention come totally into this present moment. Just be, in this present moment. Just be. Just breathe and be, here, now.

With joy and clarity open your eyes.

*****

Take a moment to reflect on the experience you just had. Listen inwards to the still, small impressions which are easily overlooked, like the ephemeral details of a dream. And now take a few minutes to write them down. Go ahead – do it. It will pay. Big time. Later in this process you will be glad you did. These first impressions in particular are quite precious.

Now that the space is prepared, we are ready to begin. Let us delve right into our inner world.

Personal Transformation

Sense of Self

This is a simple and fundamental truth: our whole life – our relationship with everyone and everything – is conditioned by the relationship we have with ourselves. When we are at peace with ourselves, we are at peace with the world. Whatever issues are unresolved within, we project into our outer life.

My spiritual background taught me to understand human beings coming to me for help 'systemically' or 'wholistically' – i.e., as whole systems, rather than as people who have a problem that needs fixing. And that's also how I taught them to understand themselves.

So, what is a systemic view of a human being?

Know Thyself – this is the sentence written above the Oracle of Delphi, the famous Greek temple of wisdom. It is the point of departure of all philosophies and religions.

A human being is a complex energy system, one which has evolved over the eons: first we developed the physical body, then the emotions, and then our mind.

Our task is to develop and refine each of these three aspects, and then to integrate them into one whole. This is an ongoing process spanning our entire lifetime.

We will now have a brief look at each of the three aspects and then set out to integrate them into one coherent whole.

For a wholistic and practical approach, we will view human beings as 'fields of consciousness' throughout this book; and all that a human being is – all our feelings, thoughts, memories, plans, skills, etc. – we will address as 'energy patterns' within this field. We learn to manage these energy patterns through the practice of meditation – first to recognize them; then to clean out whatever hinders and to build in new and better patterns; then to integrate the different parts and run the whole instrument harmoniously and effectively. Finally, to elevate it, make it radiant, and awaken our powers into usefulness.

This first part of the book is dedicated to this step-by-step process, addressing each element of our inner system and providing a series of meditative exercises to hone and empower it into the best instrument it can be.

The Physical Body

Take a moment …

*****

Feel your body. Breathe into it. Help it to relax.
Take a moment to think of your physical body as the temple of your soul.

*****

You want to keep your temple clean and in good shape.

The physical body is a system which works through habits; therefore, the wellbeing of the body is ensured through a basic maintenance routine, and it is refined through the offsetting of unhealthy habits and the establishing of healthy habits. Gradual and consistent processes work best — the body will resist direct coercion, and thus valuable energy would be wasted in conflict. To handle the physical body correctly, we need sensitivity, willpower, and patience.

Through a balanced, healthy lifestyle and a common-sense attention to the body's basic needs, we can pick up and deal with many developing troubles in the system before they manifest in illness; in this way, we can keep our physical self in relative coherence.

Take a moment …

*****

Imagine treating your body as a temple: see yourself giving it only wholesome fresh food and drink, enough high-quality sleep, a healthy sex life, an environment of safety and beauty, enough exercise, sufficient privacy and quiet, plenty of sunshine, regular relaxation, and any special care it may need. Take another moment to relish what it feels like to have a body in good condition.

*****

This exercise can profitably be done also, and perhaps especially, by people with health problems. As we will later see, to imagine ourselves in good condition – even if we are not – is a way to help us get there.

On to the next field: our emotions.

The Emotions

While our physical body is something we can see and measure, our emotional world is less graspable. This is where my 'field' theory becomes very helpful:

Take a moment …

*****

Take a moment to imagine yourself in a field or bubble, which extends half a meter beyond your physical confines in all directions. Imagine this field containing all of your feelings, which are changing all the time.

*****

Our emotions are in many ways our most complex and active part, and, therefore, the most difficult to control. They are the part which holds our wounds and fears, as well as our dearest beliefs and hopes. All these condition us and move us, through emotion, into action.

To keep our emotional field in good shape is a lifelong task. We need to first learn to understand the laws of the emotional world and to direct this great force. The first step is, as always, observation. Just sitting there and listening to the feelings.

Take a moment …

*****

Just take a minute and listen to how you feel right now.

*****

It really only takes a minute to appreciate the complexity of this seemingly simple task, and all at once we understand that we clearly need to develop some skills.

Once we learn how to observe or listen to our feelings, we become aware of their dual nature: there is always the duality of pleasure and pain, hope and fear, negative and positive feelings. So our task is dual as well: to take care of our negative feelings, which are our unfinished business, and to develop our emotional strength and wellbeing.

The emotional field of an infant is wide open, and in many ways an empty field. As we go through life, this field is filled with emotions. We see the world through the veil of these feelings. Our feelings colour our perception of the world around us, and therefore profoundly condition the quality of our life. So according to the quality of our emotions will be our life.

That's why we must pay very close attention to what is happening in our emotional field.

Not a single person in this world has had a childhood without emotional wounds and negative feelings. We all experienced many instances where something was not in resonance with our being; that can be either something done to us, or by us, or observed by us. And as a child, we don't have the tools to properly deal with strong negative feelings. They just come crashing into us. They continue to hang as incomplete emotional experiences somewhere in our field and develop into negative emotional patterns based on pain, anger, or fear for instance. As we grow up, we are left with these negative feelings – even though we often don't even remember what caused them.

A negative feeling such as fear, anger, guilt, or grief causes us to contract around it. This does not allow the energy to flow in our field; we lose our spontaneity and we don't see clearly. As a result of these contractions, we keep on making mistakes and we suffer.

To put it clearly: we stand in the way of our success.

In the beginning we run away from these painful areas in ourselves; we try to avoid them. We create a fog around them so we don't feel them. We distract ourselves. But the more we wish to take our own life in our hands, the clearer those dark spots stand out.

We gradually understand that in order to be really happy and successful, we need to address these deeply entrenched issues and do the cleansing, healing, and balancing which is needed for a free flow of energy.

Every one of our uncomfortable feelings points to an unfinished business. It can be superficial and recent, corrected easily and released quickly; but what is most difficult are the longstanding issues from early childhood. These are the ones most conditioning our lives, and these are the ones most difficult to access. Most of these relate to how much our parents or close associates could or could not love us when we were very young.

It is hugely important that we don't judge ourselves for having these negative feelings. Everybody has them; try to remember this as you face yourself. Not one person in the world is free of this. So relax and find compassion for yourself. To take care of our emotions is a lifetime task. Take one step at a time. As with everything, a problem becomes smaller the moment we turn our attention to it, although it may loom large at first glance. It is just a matter of starting this work, staying consistent, and going through with it. If there is deep and especially early trauma, you may need professional help. For spiritually oriented people, a Psychosynthesis therapy, especially in combination with meditative work, would be preferable to a conventional therapy, as it addresses the deeper and more causal layers which become relevant to an awakening person.

When we first become aware of the world of our emotions, it can be quite overwhelming. Feelings change constantly, like a kaleidoscope.

In the beginning it is almost impossible to discriminate emotionally between ourselves and our surroundings. We are constantly being influenced by the emotions of others. Every human being is in a constant process of creating emotions. Every feeling, every desire of every human being is part of the emotional atmosphere we live in.

Take a moment ...

*****

Visualize for a minute all the different emotional worlds you are a part of, each one with their special atmosphere – family, friends, work, your city, etc.

*****

In order to not get lost in all these emotional fields, we must build up our own emotional identity.

How do we do this?

In the emotional world it is all about imagination. Our imagination is to the emotional world what our muscles are in the

Awaken the Will to Love | 27

physical world. We move and change our emotions through using the imagination.

This may sound like child's play, just fantasy, but it is actually very powerful stuff.

What we imagine long and strong enough will indeed take shape inside of us. At first it is difficult to believe this. The problem is that when we don't believe in something, we are not motivated to do it.

Let's try a test trial:

Take a moment …

*****

Choose an emotional quality which you would like to build into your field – joy, courage, self-confidence, trust, serenity, or any other beautiful quality relevant to you.

The moment you choose one, if you are serious about it, it already starts to grow in you. Think about it every day. Desire it. Imagine this quality growing inside of you. Reserve judgement for one month and then review any changes.

*****

There are many meditation techniques for building new emotional patterns and habits. For the moment it is only important to realize that this is in fact possible. This means that you will be able to get a handle on your emotions, to run them instead of them running you.

Imagine!

The Mind

The third aspect of our personality is the mind. Like our emotional world, we can also imagine our mental world as a field. Both of them are part of what the universal wisdom teachings call the 'human aura'.

Take a moment ...

*****

Imagine yourself again in your bubble. This time focus on your thoughts. Imagine them like little objects of different shapes and sizes floating around you in the bubble.

*****

What we usually mean by 'mind' is the *thinking faculty*, which distinguishes man from the animals. It is our creative agent. This thinking faculty is much more complex and meaningful than realised at first glance. The following image shows Assagioli's map, his famous Egg Diagram:

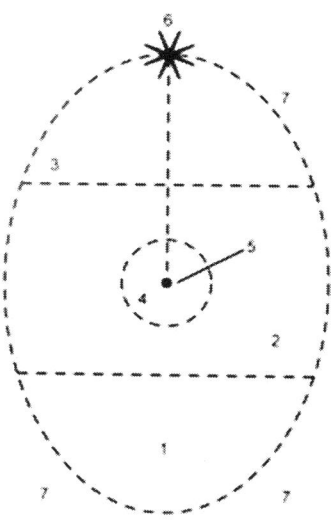

1. The Lower Unconscious
2. The Middle Unconscious
3. The Higher Unconscious or Superconscious
4. The Field of Consciousness
5. The Conscious Self or I
6. The Higher Self
7. The Collective Unconscious

We will be using a simpler map, distinguishing three different aspects: the conscious mind, the subconscious mind, and the super-conscious mind.

The conscious mind is the field of our everyday awareness. It is the intellect, the great computer which registers every stimulus and then catalogs, stores, and censures the stimuli according to our inner tendencies and beliefs. This computer makes programs in order to work out solutions and achieve envisioned aims. It is the organ of decision-making and common sense. It sits in the left hemisphere of the brain.

The subconscious mind is actually the storehouse of memory of all experiences in all lifetimes, of all the senses. It is also the seat of our beliefs. We are conditioned through these beliefs, whether we are aware of them or not.

This content stays subconscious, which means it is not available and not changeable until we willingly and with intent go down to this cellar and bring the stuff up into the daylight of our conscious mind. Only in this way can we begin to change these conditioning beliefs.

The super-conscious mind is the organ which links us to our higher wisdom. Through it we can perceive and understand higher and more abstract thoughts. This is the area where we can receive new ideas, insights, and intuitions. Through meditation we learn to build a bridge between the conscious mind and this higher mind, by stilling the conscious mind and learning to listen to the higher mind, and then downloading the higher insights into our conscious mind.

There are membranes between the three aspects of the mind, which are semi-transmitting. A healthy and developed human being has membranes which are both solid and permeable. We can get a glimpse of these membranes in the moments when we know the answer to something or have a very high insight, but we can't grasp it clearly enough to formulate it into words. Or perhaps we want to remember a dream and we can't quite grasp it. This means that something is going on in the higher mind or in the subconscious mind, but it doesn't make it through the membrane, and so the intellect cannot yet register it.

Usually we are so identified with the intellect that we are not even aware of the existence of the other two parts, even though we are conditioned by them. In order to experience the whole self, we must change this.

Unfortunately, our head is usually full of small-talk, full of inner noise which is created by the interaction between sensory input and what it triggers in all three departments of the mind. To get a handle on this situation, we again first must observe the phenomenon.

Here we come to the point in meditation that is the simplest and the most difficult at the same time:

Take a moment ...

*****

Just sit quietly and observe your mind. Direct your full attention to it for a moment now, only for one or two minutes, before reading on.

*****

If you did this seriously, you either just had a mind-blowing, wonderful experience of peace and bliss, which sometimes happens to beginners, a moment of grace; or, more likely, you were surprised and maybe even shocked by the uncontrollable activity in your brain. It is humbling to meet our inability to control what is happening in our own head. On our journey to becoming a conscious human being, there is no way around meeting this turmoil and learning to manage it.

The moment we manage to have at least a little bit of quiet in our mind, we soon realize that we can direct our thoughts consciously, and that this is a powerful way indeed to run our life.

When we start to use our mind in an active, self-directed way, we begin to experience ourselves as a mental identity. We harness our intellect and we become creative. We begin to think conscious thoughts and construct so-called '*thoughtforms*' – clusters of coherent thoughts built around a central concept (we will look deeper into their nature later on). These thoughtforms, when constructed well, become like magnets in our mental field, moving mental matter. We begin to consciously create our life.

Take a moment …

*****

Energy follows thought – take a moment to have another reflection on this premise.

*****

The Personality

According to the universal wisdom teachings, our personality is a three-fold field of consciousness, in and through which we operate in the world: the smallest is what is called the 'etheric field', which is the subtle aspect of the physical body, the so-called 'health-aura'; the next is the 'emotional field', which is a little bigger; and, finally, the 'mental field', the biggest of the three.

As we look into the inner mechanics of these three aspects, we realize that each one is a world by itself, with its own life … and often they act in a parallel way without being aware of each other.

Let us think about the physical body for a minute as a separate entity, as an animal with its own limited consciousness and agenda. The body is constantly looking for pleasure, and wants to avoid pain and effort. It wants to be in a state of wellbeing – this is what drives it.

Our emotional system – not unlike a child – is also a separate entity, with its own limited consciousness and agenda. It wants love, it wants to be praised, it wants to be entertained. And when it doesn't get what it wants, it is grumpy, angry, depressed, etc. In short, it constantly strives to feel good by pursuing certain goals and avoiding painful stimuli.

The mind can also be seen as a mechanism, with its own limited consciousness and agenda. It wants to think all the time, to build thoughtforms. It loves its little projects and issues, and is very preoccupied and identified with them.

So each of our mechanisms pursues its own agenda, and we are conscious of the one which grabs our attention most strongly: when we are extremely hungry, we are unable to care about anything else. We go for food until this need is satisfied. When we are hurt by someone, we sometimes are so identified with this pain that we can't think about anything else. And when we are concentrated on a project, we often forget that the body is hungry, or that a friend waits for us.

So while our consciousness is identifying with one aspect, we are unaware of the others. This happens automatically.

As long as this is the case, we are not in control of ourselves.

We need to come to a state in which we can decide at will where to focus our attention, instead of being unconsciously drawn here and there.

In order to succeed in life, to be creative and in control of our life, we need to learn to integrate all these aspects into one functioning whole.

When the three aspects of body, emotions, and mind work in unison and efficiently, we experience an inner integrity, a basic sense of self, a sense of: "This is who I am." This is what Assagioli calls 'personal Psychosynthesis', and what we in Hechal call 'Sense of Self'.

The following is the basic Sense of Self exercise I work with in therapy.

Personal Transformation:
Meditation 1 – Sense of Self

*****

Take a few deep breaths into the lower belly. The belly rises and falls with the breathing. Let it expand a bit. Slowly, the body relaxes and the feelings and thoughts become calm.

Sense your physical body for a moment. Be aware of your spine, from bottom to top; allow the body to subtly align itself around it. Now become aware of the space surrounding the physical body, about 10cm beyond its confines in all directions; imagine this as the etheric field, the health-aura. See if you can sense something in this area – a density, texture, or other qualities.

Now let your awareness expand to about half a metre beyond your physical confines, into your emotional field. Sense its qualities and its content.

Expand your awareness to about one metre now, to the radius of the outstretched arms. Focus on the mental contents within your personal field; they are much more subtle. Imagine the qualities and shapes of your thoughts. Imagine them like little subtle structures floating around you.

Take a moment to just sense your personal field, with all its various etheric, emotional, and mental qualities and energetic patternings. Let the field harmonise while you breathe.

Turn your attention now to the contours of your personal field, where your inner life meets the world. Now gently expand the contours; make them wider and more open to the world. Now tighten the contours; pull your field closer inwards. Sense how this strengthens and solidifies your sense of self.

Now expand your boundaries again, open to the surroundings, feel your permeability. And now gently tighten the contours again until you feel your own energy, your own sense of self. Feel your spine again for a moment, fully aligned.

Remain another moment in the experience of Sense of Self.

*****

The Power to Disidentify

> *"We are dominated by everything with which our self becomes identified. We can dominate, direct, and utilize everything from which we dis-identify ourselves."* —Roberto Assagioli

Our sense of self is created through the development and then integration of our different aspects. The more solid our sense of self, the safer it is to venture out into the world. A baby, therefore, needs the safety of a very limited environment. As we grow, so grows our field of perception, which in turn expands our sense of identity, in widening circles.

Identity is a delicate issue which we humans need to juggle. If it remains too small, it limits and even imprisons and isolates us; if it grows too wide or undefined, we don't manage to find our place in the world and to fulfil our destiny. So, you ask, how can we enjoy the solidity of a safely held field of identity while playing our full role in life?

Actually, forming an identity is a two-sided affair. Paralleling and counteracting our expanding identification from the very beginning is a process of separation, of disidentification: at age two, after being totally identified with our mother, we learn to say "No!" for the first time; and from then on we do this continuously – most notably as teenagers, where we disidentify from our parents, sometimes with considerable violence, in order to find our own identity in the world.

This interplay of identification and disidentification, of saying "Yes" and saying "No", is instinctual; it operates on an unconscious level. We can elevate it into a conscious process by an act of will. This means to both choose consciously our identifications rather than go according to default, and, when the time comes, to transcend them in favour of a more appropriate one. Such relative inner freedom is a great boon towards a successful and constructive life.

Awaken the Will to Love

To attain such inner freedom, we need to counter-balance the building of a sense of self by training the muscle of disidentification. This is what keeps us flexible and free and open for our next step of development at any one time.

Take a moment …

*****

Ponder the following: Whatever we identify with controls us. Anything from which we are able to disidentify loses its conditioning power over us.

*****

This pertains to the inner and outer life: just imagine what it would feel like to disengage from the tyranny of our constant mind-chatter, of our emotional loops, of our obsessive habits; and to free ourselves from the expectations of others, from unhealthy alliances, from the belief systems of our parents and society!

To train this 'freedom-muscle', Assagioli has devised his famous 'disidentification exercise'. The following is an adaptation of it.

Personal Transformation:
Meditation 2 – Disidentification Exercise

*****

I take a few deep breaths. Slowly I gather my consciousness inwards, into myself. Gradually I let go of the past and of the future. I come totally into this present moment. I feel my body; I sit well in it. I feel my gratitude for this wonderful instrument. I feel for a moment the different body sensations. They change all the time. I am identified with this body and its sensations. But as I observe it, I realise, this body is not who I am in my essence. I have a body, but I am not my body.

I become now aware of my feelings. I have many feelings. They change all the time. I am identified with them, but as I observe them I realise that in actuality they are not who I am in my essence. These feelings happen in me. I have feelings, but I am not these feelings.

I become aware now of my thoughts. They change all the time. I am identified with them, but as I observe them I realise that they are not who I am in my essence. These thoughts happen in me. I have thoughts, but I am not these thoughts.

I am the one who observes. I am the consciousness behind all these sensations, feelings and thoughts. I am a centre of pure self-consciousness and will.

*****

The Inner Director

We work towards building a balance between each part of our personality, and then we learn not to identify with any of them. Use them, but do not be used *by* them. Walking on these two legs establishes a new alignment, a fuller integrity.

There comes into existence an inner core self. Assagioli calls it the 'Conscious Self'. I call it the 'Inner Director'.

The Inner Director is actually a solidified sense of self, the crown of the long process of self-building, from the moment we say our first "No!" at age two, to puberty when we affirm our own values, and later around age twenty-one when we solidify our belief system (which is our mental sense of self).

When we integrate all these into one, we have what we call a 'fully integrated personality' – a central force which takes the reins of life into hand and runs the show. This Inner Director says: *I am the thinker, the feeler, the doer. I am a conscious entity. I am my own boss.* This is in actuality the birth of a new level of consciousness, and brings a new level of capacity – the capacity to gather consciousness into one single point.

Think of consciousness as a substance. Consciousness can be collected and focused or it can scatter and spread. Our usual mode of being is that our consciousness is scattered in many directions simultaneously, mostly on the periphery, identified with outer forms and events. Part of our consciousness is thinking about having a pizza, for example, at the same time that we still feel angry because of a quarrel we just had with a friend; in our mind we are already planning our evening, while simultaneously trying to remember that new app we wanted to download. We are also aware of the person on the other side of the street and even form an opinion about them. Etc., etc., the cycle goes on and on.

In order to get from this scattered consciousness into a single point of focus, we must turn to the logical place with which to collect it: the highest point of the conscious mind, at the midway point between the conscious and the super-conscious. There is an actual physical location for it: in the brain cavity. Sometimes this place is called 'the seat of the Director'. More important than the actual location, however, is the state of consciousness.

We can learn to manage ourselves and our life from this seat through meditation. A decision which is made from this inner centre is powerful. A person who is holding the reins of their life from this central position can move their consciousness at will into different areas and activities, and consequently they become successful and their field of influence becomes bigger.

It is from this new level of consciousness that we, as this Inner Director, say: 'I am a centre of pure self-consciousness and will.' It is a magical state of being – actually the most complete for a human being. It is a synthesis of the two complementing aspects of self-awareness and self-direction; of observation and will-propelled action.

It is a new platform from which we have a 360-degree view. It allows us to be aware of and to be active in three directions: inwards into our own personality, upwards towards our soul, and outwards into the world. This means that, first of all, the work on the contents of the personality becomes much more effective. Secondly, from this platform is thrown a first line of contact upwards towards the super-conscious.

When this happens the spiritual world starts to open up to us: we become aware of our own soul, or higher self, and later of other spiritual connections; telepathy and intuition are developed – the ability to tap into the realm of higher consciousness and to know things as they are from a truer and wiser vantage point, rather than as they appear through the filter of the personality.

In this space in which self-reflection occurs in two directions, transformation takes place – transformation of consciousness, of identity, of identification.

And as the result of the two, a third new dynamic starts: our will becomes activated and empowers us in our interaction with the world. We can see the wider context of any situation and are prompted to act on behalf of the common good. We become a conscious agent for change.

To build this state of the Inner Director is life-changing. It takes much preparation and practice, but it's a worthwhile investment. Before we address each of the three angles – inwards, upwards and outwards – separately, let us have a first taste of the magic of the new state of consciousness.

One simple and surprising way to experience it is by looking at what is called a '3D picture' – a computer-generated design. When looking at it with a relaxed, unfocused gaze, a three-dimensional image magically appears within the picture. Holding this image in our relaxed yet focused awareness causes our left- and right-brain hemispheres to align. This subtle state of consciousness of a calm focus resembles the state of the Inner Director. You can find many such 3D pictures on the Internet. Here is one link:

http://earthlingz.net/GALLERIES/COMPUTERGRAPHICS/STEREOGRAMS/STEREOGRAMS.html

It sometimes takes some practice, but when you get the trick, the effect is magical.

Take a moment …

*****

Try out the 3D picture. Once you succeed in seeing the three-dimensional image, observe your state of consciousness. Make a mental note of it, so that you may reproduce it later. Imagine for a moment that you are sitting in on an important negotiation in which all of the participants hold this calm focus, perhaps with the help of such a 3D picture. Imagine each of them speaking only while being able to hold this calm focus. What a beneficial negotiation that would be!

*****

See if you can replicate this calm focus within the following exercise. It is an adaptation of a classic Buddhist exercise called *The Mountain*.

Personal Transformation:
Meditation 3 – The Mountain

*****

Imagine that your body is a mountain. Feel this feeling of being a mountain. Your whole being relaxes into being a mountain. Very centred. And quiet. Feel the connection to the Earth. The wide base, solid and stable. You are actually part of the Earth. You are connected to everything.

Feel the 'mountainness'. Become aware of the centredness, the balance, the harmony with the surroundings. The solidity. The silent strength.

Take a minute to enjoy this wonderful feeling of grounded being.

As the mountain, become aware of the blue sky around you. Majestic. When thoughts come up in your mind, see them as clouds on that blue sky. Watch them pass and let them go. No effort, no judgment. Welcome them, accompany them for about 4 seconds, and then release them from your awareness, and wait for the next thought. Each time when you become aware that you forgot yourself in following a thought, gently bring your awareness back to being a mountain, silently observing the clouds.

From this space of alert stillness look out now over the world, scanning the landscape, not focusing on anything in particular. Look out while remaining solidly centred in yourself. Just hold everything you see in your spacious awareness, without being drawn into identification with anything. Hold this free consciousness, this pure self-consciousness for another moment.

Gradually reduce your field of vision and refocus in your own self. I am a centre of pure self-consciousness.

With the intention to retain the alert stillness, open your eyes.

*****

Looking Inwards – Self-Observation

The state of pure self-consciousness gives us the capacity to focus on any aspect of our being as an impartial observer. At first this doesn't seem of such importance, but it actually heralds a whole new level of being, in ourselves and in our relationships. We suddenly see what is going on behind the scenes. We are self-aware. We become aware of the psychological dynamics in ourselves: our emotional patterns, our mental constructs.

We realise how much they run our lives, without us even knowing. Now that we see, we for the first time start to have a choice in the matter. We have power over our thoughts, feelings and actions. Very quickly, we begin to realise that not only do we have a choice, but we actually are the creators of our inner reality!

When we look a little more deeply, we are quite shocked to realise that through our *inner* reality we co-create our *outer* reality! To realise that we have co-created our outer reality means to realise that we are responsible for what we create. The moment we have seen this clearly is the moment we stop being victims. We stop blaming someone else or the world for what is happening to us. We start taking responsibility for our thoughts and feelings. And this makes us into a responsible and self-directed human being.

As I'm sure you are beginning to realise, this is a lot to metabolise and actually do. But it all starts with the process of self-observation. That's why self-observation is so much more important than what it seems at a casual glance.

The act of self-observation is relatively easy; it's what this *causes* which is difficult.

When we begin observing our inner self, we are in for a long and deepening journey, one which may at times be quite wild and stormy. We meet with unexpected gremlins playing tricks on us, and with frightening sea monsters and dark figures between the rocks. The demons from our unconscious can rise and dance on the table. And this is what we must face and heal, by bringing them into the light of day, into our consciousness. When this is a conscious process, with a plan and directed by the Inner Director – that quiet observer – we always have the possibility to shift back to an eagle eye's view.

It is our platform of observation which will keep us oriented and focused during this process. The main challenge is to remember ourselves as the observer while we observe ourselves. Let us train this skill through an exercise of self-observation, an adaptation of the disidentification exercise.

Personal Transformation:
Meditation 4 – Self-Observation

*****

Take a few breaths and relax. Imagine yourself on top of a mountain. As you oversee the landscape, enter a state of alert stillness. I am a centre of pure self-consciousness.

From this platform of observation, imagine seeing yourself, somewhere down below. Take a look at your physical body. Notice the posture, and any sensations. "This is my body. And I am a centre of pure self-consciousness."

Now look closer and see if you can discern your emotions. What is this person down below feeling? Choose one emotion and observe it for a moment, without judging. Just observe. "This is an emotion happening in me. And I am a centre of pure self-consciousness."

Now let your inner eye observe your thoughts. Let the thoughts run as they will and just observe them. No judgment. Now focus in on one thought and reflect on it for a moment. "This is one of my thoughts. And I am a centre of pure self-consciousness."

Now, as the quiet observer, take a look at your personality in its entirety, assessing its state like a loving parent. What is the state of this personality? How integrated, how well-built is it? What is the next step in its development? Take note of this next step. Take a moment to feel arising in you the will to take this next step.

"I am a centre of pure self-consciousness and will."

With a sense of quiet, focused intention, open your eyes.

*****

Looking Upwards – The Soul

We have now established a platform of observation at the highest point of our personality, that eagle eye's view, from which we have a clear sight of all that lies below and from which we can manage our arising psychological contents.

While this work is ongoing, we can now explore another function of the magical place of the Inner Director: it also serves as a launch pad into higher states of consciousness. From here we turn our inner eye symbolically upwards, towards our higher self – the soul.

As the personality has three aspects – the physical, emotional and mental – so has our soul three aspects: higher light and intelligence, higher love and joy, and higher will and purpose.

In an ongoing, rhythmical, dedicated meditation practice we gradually learn to open a channel of communication through which we can contact this much higher state of consciousness, which is so much clearer, more loving and inclusive and more powerfully focused than our everyday consciousness could ever achieve.

Each time we have a successful meditation, something of this higher self quality is built into our personality. It is the Inner Director which directly benefits from this, the Inner Director which gradually becomes infused and upgraded by this higher quality. A magical transformation happens, an expansion of consciousness, of identity. It is as though a whole new layer is being added to the bandwidth of life. More light, more love and more will.

In short, a fuller sense of presence is ours.

It takes years of dedicated practice to gradually transform ourselves into a spiritual human being. Each attempt paves the way a little farther, tramples the path a little firmer. And there is the curious little exercise – one which Assagioli used to recommend as well – the Do-As-If technique; in common parlance, 'fake it until you make it'. By practicing "doing as if we are a soul", we gradually think, feel and act more in alignment with the soul.

Let us try this out in the following exercise. It is what we in the school of meditation call a full 'Personality–Soul Alignment'. Once it is learnt, it becomes the foundational daily meditation, the corner stone of our daily spiritual hygiene.

Personal Transformation:
Meditation 5 – Personality–Soul Alignment

*****

Collect your consciousness into yourself. Take a few deep breaths. Feel your physical body, and help it to get as comfortable as possible, in a relaxed uprightness.

Feel a connection with the earth through the body, a sense of being grounded and centred.

Now turn your attention to the feelings and observe them for a moment. Accept them as they are, as part of yourself. Embrace them with gentleness and softness and acceptance. Within this embrace feel them calm down.

Turn your attention to your thoughts and observe them, without judgment, without changing them; just observe. Letting the thoughts come and go.

Remember yourself as the observer. Just observe the thoughts, and release them, remaining the observer.

From your platform of observation, imagine drawing a line of light upwards, towards a ball of light about a metre above your head. This ball of light is like a little sun and it represents your soul.

Become aware of the special light of this little sun. Let it enter your mind and bring clarity into your thoughts; sense your scope of vision expand, each thought becoming clear and focused.

Now open your heart to the love of the soul. Imagine the love that you so much want, and realise that it is always available. Just open your heart now to it. Your heart fills with the love and joy of the soul.

Now invite the soul presence into your physical body, into each cell. Feel its cleansing and renewing effect as it permeates the body with a new vitality. Allow the presence of the soul to strengthen your will power and your sense of purpose and life direction.

Take a minute to just sit in this presence and wholeness. Feel yourself being radiant.

Let the soul radiance expand into your surroundings as a blessing.

With the intention to retain this radiance, open your eyes.

*****

Looking Outwards – Ready to Expand

This fullness of our being – personality and soul integration – is a wonderful state. Experiencing the radiance and clarity of the soul, even if fleetingly in the beginning, expands our perspective in an unexpected way. It gives us a much deeper experience of how we are all connected, how we are truly 'our brother's keeper'. It awakens in us a desire, a *will*, to act not only on behalf of our own interest but on behalf of the common good.

It is in this sense that "spiritual" equals "transpersonal": we go beyond the personal; in essence, we start living not only for ourselves. We want to become active in the world, consciously. We want to play a constructive role.

That's where the Inner Director, in addition to being a 'centre of pure self-consciousness', becomes a 'centre of will' as well. Our platform serves us now to project our inner will outwards, to take action in the world, in a conscious way.

Every human being has a will; but for the most part it remains instinctual and unconscious, active only for self-preservation. It can and must be recruited into conscious use by the Inner Director.

This vital human function is little dealt with in mainstream psychology. Assagioli introduced it as a central trait to be recognised and consciously developed. The will is like an intricate system of muscles to be trained; it has different aspects and phases. It is the conscious and skilful employment of our will which is at the root of making conscious choices, and thereby consciously creating our lives. It is the will which makes the difference between floating along the evolutionary path and becoming conscious co-creators. Since Assagioli has written a whole book about the training of the will (*The

Act of Will), I will not go into it further here, but I highly recommend its study.

From now on, for the rest of the book we will turn our attention to the manifestation of our inner coherence and empowerment in our lives and the wider world. The different segments will from now on be accompanied with illustrations from my own experience. The first ring of expansion involves entering a conscious relationship with another human being.

Relationship

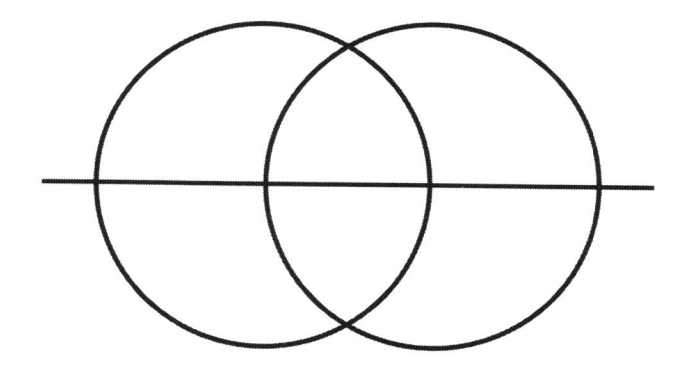

The above symbol, called *Vesica Piscis*, is a central building-block in sacred geometry. It underlies many ancient traditions and connotes right relations.

In this symbol we see two spheres overlapping. Each sphere represents a coherent, independent personal field, entering into a free yet committed relationship with another coherent field. The integrity of each sphere is kept, while the responsibility for the coherence of the common space is mutually taken.

Take a moment ...

*****

Contemplate the symbol and realise the relationship of the two spheres.

*****

The horizontal line signifies the bond of the heart, which remains intact even if the two spheres should at some point decide to move to some distance, to have less overlap, less common space or even to move out of each other's personal lives.

This picture of relationship makes for integrity. I love this symbol. I have had the privilege twice to use it when I acted as the officiating celebrant in the wedding ceremonies of friends. In a symbolic act, both bride and groom took a step into right relation with each other, retaining their sense of self and at the same time committing to the sacred union of marriage.

The following exercise can be used for observing and regulating any type of relationship.

Personal Transformation:
Meditation 6 – Relationship

*****

Choose a personal relationship you want to work with.

Start by first concentrating on yourself.

Take a few deep breaths and relax. Imagine yourself standing within your personal field. Feel your feet solidly on the ground. Feel your spine. For a moment sense your personal field in its entirety, your bubble. Sense the contours of it. Feel your presence solid and coherent.

As you invite the other person into your presence, dedicate this meeting to the highest good of all. Visualise him or her approaching, coming to a comfortable distance opposite you, not too close and not too far. Put aside now everything you know about the person and your common history. See this person as a field of energy, a sphere. And take a moment to just observe, allowing for new and perhaps surprising perceptions.

Now turn your attention to yourself, to your own field. What is happening in it in response to the proximity of this other field? Allow yourself to become very receptive. No judgment, no analysing at this stage. Just sensing.

Adjust the distance between you to suit your comfort as you observe.

Listen to any pictures, memories, body sensations, etc., until you feel you have received all the information needed or possible at this time.

Release the other respectfully, into the hands of their own soul.

Focus now back in your own field; allow a moment to feel the after-effect of the meeting.

Then release these effects and gently but firmly re-establish your own frequency in your field and affirm your own sense of self. If needed, tighten your aura a bit for solidification.

As you return to full waking consciousness and while the impressions are still fresh, take a moment to write them down.

*****

White Magic

We can now expand beyond one relationship into the greater sphere of our life. We want to try out these new tools we have developed so that we can live a conscious life and become a creative agent in the world. This is clearly a lifetime task.

By now we have sufficiently observed our personality, so we have a rough idea of what is going on, what liabilities and resources we possess. And we have established a first thread of communication with our soul. Now we need to bring the two together for positive action in the world. This is actually a science; in the universal wisdom teachings it is called 'White Magic'.

Magic here refers to using your mind and will to change the world, and *White* signifies that it comes from a pure heart, guided by the soul. By using our will effectively, we become a magician; to have the soul control this process makes us into a white magician. To put it more plainly, this means to employ both our will and our heart to take responsibility for all aspects of our life, for our sphere of influence, and become a conscious creative agent within it for the highest good of all involved.

By now we already know that each new process needs to start with observation; now we will do an exercise for becoming aware of our sphere of influence.

Take a moment …

*****

'Sphere of Influence' – just to think about this term is already evocative.

*****

Personal Transformation:
Meditation 7 – Sphere of Influence

*****

Breathe and relax. Feel your spine and allow the body and the whole personal field to align around it. Project a line of light upwards to the soul. Let the light and love and will of the soul infuse your entire being. Collect your consciousness into one point. 'I am a centre of pure self-consciousness and will.'

From this platform of the Inner Director, take a look at your field of influence as it is at this moment of your life.

Start with the physical plane. What physical space and physical objects are you responsible for? Do you take good care of this field of influence? Is it too big for you or too small, or is it just right? To what degree do you have your physical world in order?

Radiate your light and your love and your will into this sphere of influence.

Now focus on your emotional world, which is the world of relationships. Get a sense of this aspect of your sphere of influence. Recall your relationships – to family, friends, colleagues, to casual online encounters.

Do you take full responsibility for this field of influence? Does it have the right size? To what degree does it express the qualities of the heart, like beauty, love and joy?

Radiate a heart blessing into this field of influence.

Turn now to your mental field of influence. What mental impact do you have on your surroundings? How are your thoughts, ideas, opinions, statements, influencing the people around you? Are you taking full responsibility for this influence? How big is your mental reach? To what degree do you express mental clarity and purpose? Radiate your clarity into your mental field of influence.

Assume now the position of the Inner Director overseeing and caring for all areas of your life expression.

Feel the soul's light, love and will pour through you into your whole sphere of influence.

*****

Subtle Patterns

As we live our life more and more as the soul-infused Inner Director, something happens to our perception: we become more sensitive and receptive. We pick up more subtle aspects of objects and people around us. So-called extra-sensory perception (ESP), for example, telepathy, psychometry or premonition, becomes part of our experience. While at the beginning this can create considerable discomfort, confusion and, sometimes, real trouble, once we learn how to handle this expanded awareness it becomes a great gift for ourselves and a service to others.

In response to this need I devised the 'Psychic Investigation' course, a training program for my students to manage and develop their ESP, according to the principles laid down by Alice Bailey under the heading of *Higher Psychism*. This training includes a technique for using our higher senses on behalf of others.

The refinement of our inner senses brings to our awareness subtle underlying patterns in ourselves and in the world. Separate incidents are seen in wider contexts, and in wider time-frames. Underlying the apparently random incidents in our lives, an unsuspected lawfulness starts to reveal itself. Cycles and rhythms are noticed both in our inner dynamics and in the world. And, of course, we become immediately interested in cooperating intelligently with them rather than paying the price of clashing with them.

For me, it started at age sixteen, when my mother pointed out to me that I seem to cry at each full moon. Going through my journal, which I had already kept for a few years, I noticed the moon's profound effect on my emotional life. From that moment on I started to observe myself during the lunar cycle. I noticed that towards the full moon, life seemed to grow much more intense: I had more energy in my physical system, to the extent that sometimes it was hard to sleep; my feelings were more dramatic; and my mental processes were accelerated.

It took a number of years to find out that I can at least partially direct this intensity, use it for my own purposes rather than being driven by it: I learnt to concentrate my efforts on my meditative life at the full moon's approach, and as a result of it my meditations became much deeper and more significant.

With the years I noticed more cycles. For example, the monthly cycle of the astrological influences. I taught myself to comply with them, to use them, much like we use different weather conditions for different activities.

The universal wisdom teachings provide profound tools for understanding and utilising the underlying energies and cycles which condition our existence. While most people interested in self-development are familiar with astrology, there is another tool which I want to introduce here, because it has helped me and my students in very practical ways. It is called 'The Seven Rays', which I briefly mentioned earlier. This model basically states that there are seven distinct energies which underlie all of creation; these seven rays, or rates of vibration, create all there is in cyclic interplay and in divine law and order.

This model is used to analyse vast time periods – and solar systems, planets, kingdoms of nature, nations – down to the microcosm of the human being. In fact, it serves as the basis for a comprehensive science of esoteric psychology developed by Alice Bailey. According to Bailey, each human being is conditioned by a combination of these seven rays.

Assagioli adopted and simplified this model, calling it 'Typology'. Here are the keywords for the seven types:

Will
Love
Intelligence
Beauty
Knowledge
Enthusiasm
Organisation

These keywords are only meant to give a general first glimpse. In no way do they do justice to the profundity of these energies.

In the same way as the attempt to understand the astrological qualities playing through us causes us to look at ourselves from a more systemic angle, the 'trying on' of the different Ray types and realising which one is conditioning us and which ones it would be good to cultivate can be very revealing.

For my advanced students I devised a year-long process of self-investigation according to this Seven Rays model, including some basic astrology. Such investigation takes us beyond 'content-management', which conventional psychology provides by concentrating on the emotional and mental patterns – our psychological content; rather, the Seven Rays model addresses the structure, quality and refinement of the personal field itself – viewing it as an instrument through which archetypal energies are flowing. To lift our eyes from the contents to get a systemic view makes it possible to develop ourselves systematically, not just in reaction to ever-arising issues.

We cannot go deeper into astrology and typology or Ray-ology here, but we will meet them again in the context of a group. I strongly recommend you investigate these models of reality further, as they bring the understanding of our own and others' character, behaviour and roles in life to a whole new level.

There is no end to developing and refining our personal field. While this process necessarily continues throughout our lives, let us now enlarge our vision. We are ready for a very exciting leap – from the personal field to the group field.

The Group as a Transformation Tool

A Word about Groups

Groups have always played an important role for human beings – the most fundamental of which being the family and tribal unit, which used to be the frame of reference from the beginning to the end of life. This type of cohesion based on bloodline and herd instinct is losing its appeal in the modern civilisation; this is due to the fact that we don't need it anymore for survival and we have become more individualised in our consciousness.

This faces us with much more of a choice about our identity and sense of belonging. It brings freedom, but also requires a different, more awake form of consciousness, particularly if we don't want to get lost in a world where the known structures are quite rapidly disappearing.

New types of belonging are forming, from family WhatsApp groups to bigger and bigger global alliances. Overall, they seem to be based more on function than on heredity. These functions span a wide spectrum, from conservative to visionary: first, there are those groups whose purpose it is to build and maintain the basic structures of society, which include most professional work systems. Then there are the recreational groups, the many clubs and groups forming around common hobbies. Lastly there are the growing number of initiatives which take on the care for some part of society which needs mending or improving; these are, the many non-profit organisations which sometimes are called the 'goodwill groups'. At the edge of that end of the spectrum there are the curious small groups of pioneers which open themselves to the new ideals, the new values which are entering human horizons. These so-called transformation groups are trying out a new level of consciousness and new models of being.

Any group is a great arena for creativity and growth, both individually and collectively. However, transformation groups in particular can facilitate a new level of consciousness for its members. They are growth catalysts. Most importantly, in these pioneering groups the common space is used to try out something new together instead of only as an individual. The attention is turned to the group as an entity by itself – a larger field of consciousness. It becomes the laboratory, not only for trying out individual new behaviour, but also for trying out new ways of being and acting together as a group entity; actually experimenting with models of the future for human living. Group life – group consciousness – is truly the new frontier for humanity.

I have always been attracted to working in the context of such a group. From my universal spirituality studies, I knew that at the present threshold on which humanity finds itself, to a new astrological cycle or age, that of Aquarius, research of the laws underlying group life are of vital relevance. Group consciousness is one of the key features of Aquarius. Being born in the sign of Aquarius myself, I had yearned for such an opportunity for a long time.

When a group of my senior students completed the training of Psychic Investigation after more than five years in my school, I felt it time to invite them to become colleagues, to form a group of equals and to start building something together.

Now began a fascinating journey into a whole new level of being. As we will see, the process of the individual work is repeated and multiplied ten-fold on the level of the group. First we have the 'looking inwards' – understanding the inner dynamics within the group field. We 'look upwards', contemplating the group purpose.

And when the group reaches enough solidity, it starts to 'look outwards', taking on a greater role in a wider context.

The same laws apply here, only naturally much more complex and far-reaching. I was and still am fascinated by these group laws.

The following chapter touches upon these laws and gives examples from our group life in Jerusalem and offers some exercises. If you are part of a transformation group, you can use these exercises by either actually performing them with the group or doing them alone (but still with your group in mind); if you are not at present part of such a group, you can work with an imaginary group – perhaps it will inspire you to initiate one yourself! I heartily recommend it. Group life is such a huge accelerator of personal development. A group as an entity can do what individuals cannot. Working consciously together, in small and big groups, we create islands of coherence, and this coherence will spread into the wider collective in which we find ourselves.

Allow me to share a fiery quote by Ken Wilber about the transformative power of groups:

> *"Let small pockets of radically transformative spirituality, authentic spirituality, focus their efforts, and transform their students. And let these pockets slowly, carefully, responsibly, humbly, begin to spread their influence, embracing an absolute tolerance for all views, but attempting nonetheless to advocate a true and authentic and integral spirituality – by example, by radiance, by obvious release, by unmistakable liberation. Let those pockets of transformation gently persuade the world and its reluctant selves, and challenge their legitimacy, and challenge their limiting translations, and offer an awakening in the face of the numbness that haunts the world at large."* —Ken Wilber

The Group Field

Take a moment …

*****

Imagine yourself in a group. Feel the group as a space or field, containing all the feelings and thoughts of the group members.

*****

The truth is that the group is an entity that is much fuller than an individual can ever be. In its development it goes through the same phases as a person – only they are far more complex and intense. The group heart is composed of the blending of the hearts of all group members, and so is the group mind a synchronisation of the minds of all group members, and likewise is the group soul the higher point of synthesis and purpose gleaned from the highest levels of consciousness of the group members.

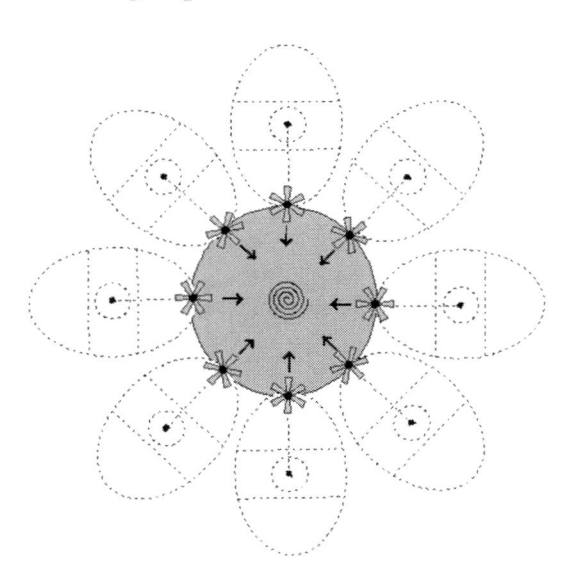

The above diagram is taken from the Group Focaliser Course of the Community of Living Ethics. Each sphere symbolises one group member. Just by looking at this diagram one immediately realises that the process of integration of a group entity requires more complex rules and techniques. There are many aspects which need to be attended to. The emotional and mental states of each group member affects the group field as a whole, and the various relationships between group members add richness to the group dynamics.

Issues naturally arise in any group. In a healthy group, they are consciously and constructively dealt with. This sounds easy enough when it is written in one sentence like the above, but, as everybody who has ever tried it knows, in practice much trial and error and much maturity is required to handle and steer the different energies in a group of the new type. A transformation group is an accelerator for personal growth, bringing to the surface our individual patterns, activating them as they rub against each other in full view.

Therefore, a group must find a mechanism for bringing up the group issues and dealing with them, similar but much more intense than in the individual sphere. In order to keep the group field clean and healthy and harmonious, it is best to dedicate specially scheduled sessions for this process. The more mature the group members, the easier it is to deal with the constantly arising psychological content of the transformation.

I can see in retrospect that I laid the groundwork for our new transformation group during the Teachers Training course which I taught to my new colleagues. I called this course 'Deep Blue'. Deep Blue is the colour associated with the Second Ray of Love. Love is the quality underlying the work of healing, therapy and teaching, and all that pertains to the establishment and maintenance of right relations in general. It is also the quality and substance out of which a group field is built. It includes such skills as listening, also to what is left unsaid; sharing respectfully and significantly; responding to others without judgement, from the heart; remaining stable in one's centre within the energies of the group, etc.

While the learning of these skills was needed for the new teachers to hold their own courses, this was great preparation also towards the establishment of our own core group. They were invaluable in dealing with all kinds of interpersonal issues which naturally arose once we began planning a common project.

Complementing these skills of right relations is group meditation. Nothing is more effective in aligning the different energies and weaving the group into one whole than regular group meditation. Let us take another look at the group diagram above, and then take it into meditation.

Group Transformation:
Meditation 1 – The Group Field

*****

Breathe and relax. Become aware of your personal field. Allow the physical, emotional and mental components to come into coherence. Let the soul infuse the personal field with its light, love and will. As you prepare to enter into a larger field of a group, adjust the boundaries of your personal field – adopt the right tightening to allow you to retain a solid sense of self while opening yourself to the group members.

Now allow into your consciousness the presence of the group. Visualise the other group members as fields of consciousness, each with their varied contents.

Take a moment to allow the individual fields to meet and blend into one whole: see the emotional patterns rub against each other and slowly harmonise into a unified group heart. Now see the different thought patterns of the participants start to align and synchronise into one group mind. There is now one unified group field.

Visualise a brilliant ball of light above the group, symbolising the combined higher wisdom of the group members.

See this higher wisdom infuse the group field, harmonising and strengthening it. Remain a moment within the embrace of the group field.

*****

The Group Purpose

Take a moment …

*****

Imagine above the group a point of light, representing the group purpose.

*****

While for an individual this may be less pronounced and less urgent, in a group a clear purpose is vital for its survival. Most of the diverse groups in the world have a very clear purpose. There is a common interest – be it a basic need, a recreational or educational common interest or a humanitarian issue that is close to the group members' hearts. With a transformation group, because of its pioneering state, things are less clear and group purpose is therefore a continuous process of inquiry. By definition a transformation group is at the frontier of human experience, continuously peeking over the horizon and adapting itself to new visions. So the purpose of a transformation group is in constant development.

This fact causes a tension which is inherent in all transformation groups: that between the old established way of doing things and the new ideas that are sensed, but still too vague to be implemented. It is the tension between the actual and the ideal – the inner knowledge that we need to do things differently, but we don't know yet how to do it. On the threshold of the new age, to consciously stand in this tension may be the best we can do.

Group purpose, for a transformation group, is intricately related with group identity.

The purpose of our new group, for example, was to run our spiritual school together. We offered classes of meditation and self-development to diverse groups within the Jerusalem landscape:

Jews, Muslims, Christians, secular people, teenagers, bereaved parents, Jewish and Arab peace-workers, etc. Our monthly full-moon meditation meetings began to grow in size and impact.

Now that my colleagues had joined me, we needed a name and a structure. We founded a new legal entity, one which I have mentioned often in this book – namely, the Hechal Centre for Universal Spirituality in Jerusalem.

We were very happy and proud and excited to be an official non-profit organisation. But to hold our new identity appropriately to our purpose and in our environment proved to be tough for the young Hechal; we grappled with it over many years. It started right during our beautiful Hechal inauguration ceremony, which we held on the magnificent Leo full moon night of 2004 on the Mount of Beatitude. Sitting in the sacred stone circle overlooking the Sea of Galilee and the huge full moon rising from the Golan Heights onto the lake, I had inwardly heard the very clear injunction:

No more heavy temple!

Yes, there were enough heavy temples in Jerusalem. We all had an instinctive fear to drown in heavy matter, to create another 'sect', another dogma, another specialness which would just add more separation to the divisions of the City of Peace.

Our resulting reticence to play a public role in this made it difficult for us as a group to sound our note clearly enough, to hold our flag high enough to have an impact on our environment reflecting our dedication, effort and authentic medicine for what ails this place.

We were well aware that this was not only our own inability; here, in Jerusalem – a prototypal fertile place for mushrooming heavy temples – we were participating at the frontier of humanity's struggle to open to a new way. The margin between holding our form strongly enough to have a recognisable existence between all the heavy temples, and yet lightly enough to let the new light shine through us, was so very thin that it seemed not possible as yet to get it right. This issue remained a constant tension and needed a constant delicate listening to our purpose.

This delicate listening is done in a regular meditation dedicated to this end. After such a meditation the group members share their impressions. Eventually this practice results in the formulation of a concise statement pertaining to the group's goals for the short- and the long-term. In consecutive meditations this purpose statement is substantiated and refined, and it grows with the group's process.

Group Transformation:
Meditation 2 – The Group Purpose

*****

Prepare your personal field for group work by aligning your physical, emotional and mental aspects into one whole. Adjust your boundaries.

Now see yourself as part of the group. Get adjusted to the group field. Attune your heart to the group heart; synchronise your mind with the group mind. Open yourself now to the point of light above the group, symbolising the group soul. Focus in on the aspect of the soul which holds the purpose of the group. Start by bringing into your consciousness the group purpose as it is at present formulated or intuited. Reach as clear and concise a thought about it as is possible at this moment.

Now release this formulation and open your consciousness to any new impressions from the higher wisdom and will of the group. Take a moment in silence for this subtle sensing. Gradually return to everyday consciousness and try to capture your impressions.

*****

The Group Focaliser

In a group, just as for an individual, when there is an Inner Director there is also a clearer sense of purpose.

What is the Inner Director for the individual is (traditionally) the group leader for the group.

While in most groups in the world there still is one charismatic leader who steers the group, and much depends on this one leader, in the newer types of groups this model is no longer working so well. There is an urge towards group leadership and towards some form of democratic or consensual decision-making. However, in this present transition period from individual to group, we are not fully there yet. We are still struggling to invent a new type of group Conscious Self. We sense new possibilities, but also experience much painful confusion during this process.

There is often a high degree of tension between the group members' ingrained expectations towards the founder of the group according to the known rules of firm and clear leadership, and those forces within the group which call for 'democracy' – or group consensus – in line with the new Aquarian consciousness.

This tension between the old model and a new model was rather dramatic in the early Hechal group process as well. In the beginning I, as the group leader, continued to spoon-feed my former students and to provide all the direction. They were quite comfortable with this state – I had been, after all, their instructor for the last handful of years – but I actually longed for equal partners. At some point I started to revolt and to upset the status quo. As a result of my pushing for a more 'Aquarian group', towards a consensus mode of decision-making and of taking equal responsibilities, the group broke, and, sadly, many members left. After a process of painful deliberations, the remaining members decided to adopt the model of 'Group Focalisation', which was developed by our colleagues and mentors at the Community of Living Ethics in Italy (http://www.comunitadieticavivente.org/).

In this model there still is one person who steers the group, but rather than being a traditional leader who imposes their own will on the group, he or she is more of a steward who wields the group energies according to the group purpose decided upon by the group as a whole. It clearly is a transitional model, helping transformation groups at the present threshold between an old age and a new one. The focaliser, who is usually the founder of the group, acts as a Conscious Director on behalf of the group. He or she keeps the group field coherent and steers the group activities in alignment with the decided purpose.

Under the mentoring by our Italian colleagues who became close friends in the process, this model became for us like a glove on the hand.

The group focaliser possesses a magic which is similar to the magic that is unleashed when the individual person reaches the state of consciousness of the Inner Director. Like the Inner Director, the group focaliser looks inwards into the group field and holds it in coherence through his or her love, and he or she looks upwards to the group soul, actually remains in constant communion with the group soul to ascertain and keep up-to-date the purpose and direction of the group. This calls for the function of the will. The group focaliser is the custodian of the group's will. For this, he or she needs to stand firmly in his or her own will.

The group focaliser combines and synthesises in him or herself a horizontal care for the group field and a vertical connection to the higher will and purpose of the group.

Group Transformation:
Meditation 3 – The Group Focaliser

*****

Visualise yourself as the focaliser of your group. Consecrate your heart to the wellbeing of the group field.

Take a moment to just feel the group field, containing each one of the group members and the relationships between them. Embrace this whole field in your heart, harmonising it, bringing love and care to the areas which need it. Make it coherent and cohesive through your love.

Now stand firmly in your own will. Feel your own willpower and consecrate it to the highest good of the group.

Align yourself to the higher will of the group, which is held in the group's soul. Listen to any impressions. Hold the clearest thought about the group's highest purpose. Endeavor to embody this purpose and transmit it telepathically into the group field. Imbue the group field with it.

Visualise each group member coming into alignment with this purpose and moving in harmony with the others towards its fulfilment.

*****

Group Coherence through the Seven Rays

We saw that the group focaliser holds the overall responsibility for the group's purpose, which has been decided not by him or her but by the group as a whole.

When a group has a defined purpose and a directing model, the decision-making process becomes clear and a basic overall functioning is established. This corresponds to the stage where the individual has established his or her Inner Director who can regulate the personality and also receive inspiration from the soul. It is the phase where there is enough stability for the focus to shift from taking care of constantly arising issues to refining the instrument itself.

As in the individual process so also in the group, from this state of relative solidity and observation we start to discern more subtle patterns. We become aware of the more subtle energies flowing through the group; we can now apply ourselves to use and direct them.

The model of the Seven Rays (which we have briefly met already in the personal field) is of tremendous help in managing the group dynamics effectively and harmoniously and refining the group as an instrument. In a group, these Seven Rays or types work out as seven different group functions. Each member chooses one of these ray energies and cultivates it and works to embody its quality to make it available to the group. This has a regulating effect on the group dynamics. It is as if the colours in a prism or in a rainbow are suddenly put in order, and beauty and efficiency are established.

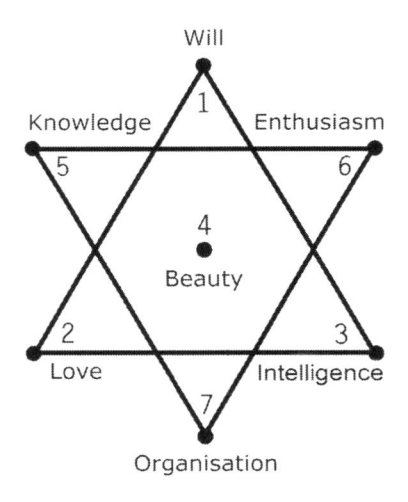

```
                    Will
                     •
                    /1\
         Knowledge /   \ Enthusiasm
              •___/_____•
              \5 /       \ 6/
               \/    4    \/
               /\    •    /\
              /  \ Beauty /  \
             /2   _____/   3\
            •_____\  7 /_____•
           Love     \  /    Intelligence
                     \/
                     •
                Organisation
```

This model was conceived by the Italian esoteric philosopher Enzio Savoini and has been extensively developed by a group of researchers in Italy (http://theplanetarysystem.org/). It is an intriguing, transforming and empowering work, the depth of which is impossible to describe in just a few sentences; it must be experienced. Our friends from the Community of Living Ethics have introduced us to this amazing science of group work. More and more transformation groups all over the planet are currently experimenting with it.

I will only very briefly state how these seven basic energies or qualities work out as group functions: the first Ray of Will takes on the role of holding the group's purpose clear and fresh; the second Ray's function is to ensure a continuous flow of love in the group field, to hold all relations well-oiled; the third Ray's function plans the various activities of the group, and it is helped by the rest of the rays, with the fourth providing the harmony and integrity between all aspects, the fifth building the structures, the sixth adding enthusiasm and motivational push; and the seventh brings it all together into one smooth operation.

Each group member takes on both the inner quality and the outer practical expressions of their chosen Ray. This works like magic. Group tensions and confusions are alleviated, and the energies are blended into a harmonious group function. The embodying of a ray function aligns the energies of each member and relates them harmoniously to all other group members. This works for small as well as for large groups, where multiple members take on the same ray function.

I don't want to give the impression that this process is always simple and straightforward. It all depends, as earlier stated, on the relative maturity of the group members. The more aligned and integrated they are, the easier is the group work.

By concentrating on the adopted ray qualities and functions rather than on the different personality patterns of the group members, much of the usual confusion and conflict of clashing personalities takes care of itself or is simply not present. When working with the personal field, we have seen the same process: when one moves the focus from the content to the actual structure, the psychological drama lessens.

There are always issues and relationships which need attention, but when working with this model the group has a map and a compass.

Take a moment …

*****

Contemplate the diagram of the Seven Rays, with the keywords for the seven qualities and their geometric inter-relation.

Choose one ray. Open yourself to sense the quality of this ray streaming into you. Feel it radiating from you now into your group, to the benefit of all.

*****

The Group as an Instrument for the Common Good

When the group energies are unified and aligned, the group seems to become like a magnet which starts to radiate – again, in much the same way as an individual. When integrated and aligned, it is noticed within its surroundings.

The new group radiance is expressed first of all in the personal lives of the group members: the heightened state of consciousness which is experienced in the group radiates out into each group member's sphere of influence. In addition to living more radiantly their daily lives, the contents, techniques and higher states of consciousness are brought through them into their respective professional fields, such as education, therapy, business, art, etc. When this happens, the group is ready to take on a bigger role. This can reveal itself in meditation by an expanding or changing sense of purpose, and also by receiving a request, a call for help, from the environment: it was our project of Psychic Investigation which unexpectedly received some interest. In our weekly meetings of psychic research, we had up until now taken as an object of observation a single human being. Now different groups – either a family, company or non-profit organisation – asked for assistance in assessing a burning situation. One of them was an anthroposophical elementary school in Jerusalem which turned to us for help with one of their classes, in which a very difficult and complex dynamic continued to play itself out over several years. Five of us went to meet their collegium and together with them we held a psychic investigation.

A psychic investigation is a structured process of observation and reflection, done from a soul-aligned inner state. A group, when soul-aligned, can act as a telepathic field, into which exceptionally comprehensive information can be received. Through a controlled process of sharing our subtle impressions and together interpreting them, we helped the team of teachers to understand the underlying dynamics and henceforth handle the class situation wisely.

As has been the case so far, as for an individual so also for a group – its field of influence grows in accordance with its inner stability and alignment.

While working psychically in service of different groups was quite a step in itself, it proved actually to be only preliminary groundwork for a much bigger step: working with a collective field.

Let us prepare ourselves for this big leap with a key exercise from our Hechal group work: the Group Alignment. This exercise is for a group what the Personality–Soul Alignment is for the individual: it is the basic spiritual group hygiene; it keeps the group healthy and at its best. The following adapted version is geared to prepare us for the collective work we are about to enter. It contains a Mantram by Alice Bailey which we sometimes use in our work.

Group Transformation:
Meditation 4 – Group Alignment

*****

We breathe and relax. We allow all the aspects of our being to come into alignment – physical, emotional, mental, personality and soul.

Now we reach out to each other with our heart. We feel all hearts blend into one unified group heart.

We open our minds to each other and allow a telepathic interplay to weave all minds into one magnetic mental field.

Together we open up to the group soul, envisioning it as a ball of brilliant light above the group. We take a moment to just sit under its inspiration. We feel the warmth of the group soul weave all hearts closer together.

We align with the will of the group soul and note how it guides and directs the group's activities.

We see our group radiant, ready to take on a service for a greater whole.

*****

We now dedicate ourselves to the task at hand:

In the centre of all love, we stand.
From that centre, we, as souls, will outwards move.
From that centre, we, the ones who serve, will work.
May the love of the Divine Self be shed abroad,
in our hearts, through our group, and throughout the world.

Collective Transformation

About Collective and National Fields

Human actions create larger and larger effects, dangerously preceding the required consciousness to understand and take responsibility for these effects. The resulting crisis has become planet-size. To rise to this occasion we must match it in consciousness; the transformation must be planet-size as well. There is no other choice.

What follows is a vision of what is possible if we expand and apply the principles and practices covered on the personal- and group-level also to the wider collective.

There are no clear-cut boundaries between a group and a collective. For our purposes, however, let us define a group as a unit of people with individual relationships, and a collective as a much larger unit in which people don't personally know each other, although they share the same characteristics. Every grouping, every cross section of humanity, is a collective. There are collectives we are born into, like our gender, ethnicity, religion or nationality, and there are groupings we choose later in life, like our profession or any interest group.

Each collective can be seen as a field of consciousness, with the same components as a person and a group: physical, emotional, mental and soul. Whether we are aware of it or not, the various collective fields have an influence on us, and the more aware we are of their existence and influence the more we in turn can exert influence on them.

A collective into which we are born is typically more ancient and complex than one that we have chosen later in life; it also holds more of a charge for us, because we are more instinctually identified with it. This applies especially for the national collective. Depending on where we are born, our national identity can have a strong conditioning effect on us – which is mostly unconscious, as we will see later. Citizens of nations with a strong tribal component have typically a stronger sense of national identity and are more deeply conditioned by it. The Jewish people, for example, have an extremely strong sense of collective belonging, for various reasons. But the present great national and international upheavals everywhere confront the citizens of all nations with the need to face their national identity in new ways; this crisis gives us an unprecedented opportunity to become aware of these larger wholes and participate in them more consciously.

Take a moment …

*****

'Sense' yourself being part of your nation. Is it pleasant? Does it feel safe and empowering? Does it feel restrictive or overpowering? Remain a moment within it and yet remember to be yourself.

*****

A nation, as stated above, is only one form of collective. Because both Hechal's and Assagioli's research focused on this aspect of the collective work, we will concentrate on it as a case study throughout the following chapter; however, the principles put forth can be applied to other collectives as well.

Hechal's First Experience with a Collective Field

In Hechal's work we stumbled unawares into a collective field.

It all began when I kept noticing in my meditation classes my students' coming up against the question of their Jewishness. How is meditation and universal spirituality related to being Jewish? Is it okay for a Jew to meditate, to open to a different spirituality?

Together with a colleague in Hechal, who is a scholar of Jewish studies, we opened a one-year course of inquiry into the seamline between Judaism and Universal Spirituality. We decided to call it *Bridge of Compassion*. My colleague would bring Jewish elements, mainly through text study; and I would bring elements from universal spirituality, mainly through guided meditations.

The first thing we did was to build a solid group field, since for this touchy subject a very safe space was needed. We started each weekly class with a meditation geared to this end, fostering love, compassion, tolerance, patience and all the beautiful qualities of the heart, and we established safe rules for sharing.

This gave the participants the opportunity to explore their own Jewishness in a loving, supportive environment. They could dare to ask the deepest and most painful and frightening questions about their Jewish identity: *What is Jewishness for me? Is there anything in me which is not Jewish? Is that okay? Am I fundamentally different from anyone else? Where am I like everyone else, just a human being?*

These questions may not seem very threatening or even relevant for citizens of other nations, who carry their national identity more lightly, but for many if not most Jewish people this type of question shakes them at the core of their being.

This course caused part of the students to painfully deconstruct their identification with their Jewishness in order to give their humanness precedence. Others found their way back to their Jewish roots and made peace with them.

The recognising and facing of national patterns and how we take part in them became the main focus of the course. The diversity of the participants and the loving, safe group field enabled us to discover and face our own national shadows; to come to the realisation that we all participate in the national patterns, that we all hold aspects of them and that our group brothers and sisters have theirs, which may not necessarily be the same as ours.

By reflecting and sharing with others, we help each other to recognise and face these national patterns, and we join forces to heal and dissolve them in ourselves.

My German background as well as my collaboration with my colleagues in my esoteric studies made me sensitive to these national patterns also among Non-Jews. I became aware of the discomfort and helplessness of many people of goodwill when it comes to the Jewish question. There are underlying issues, pushed out of the sphere of consciousness, which make it difficult to form a clear and constructive opinion and approach to the Jewish people. Inherited beliefs, guilt feelings, anger, repulsion, jealousy, etc., keep many well-meaning people in a kind of suspense and unintended alienation towards Jews. These were the same national patterns, only experienced from the outside. So I felt the need to start this bridge of compassion from the opposite end as well.

Over the following years I offered *Bridge of Compassion* presentations and workshops across Europe and America for groups of non-Jews. When meeting their feelings towards Jews, they were often taken by surprise by what was hiding beneath the surface of their consciousness.

These encounters made me realise that the Jewish people in general and Israel in particular hold more of the shadow of the West than is realised. That is the reason why it is so difficult for Western people to think objectively concerning the Jewish issue: we have the unresolved past of Europe and North America related to Christianity, the crusades, materialism in general, colonialism, the Holocaust and the creation of the state of Israel. Even if we are not aware at all about this specific issue in our personal lives, chances are that once we are confronted with it, surprisingly strong feelings may arise. It is good and healing to become aware of them. We need to understand and accept that we are part of the world, and any strong issue happening in the world will echo within us even if our personal life is not directly related to it.

Together we courageously discovered the collective anti-Semitic shadows lurking unbeknownst in the best and most spiritual people – myself included. Many participants expressed their gratitude and relief that this delicate and disturbing issue could be touched in such a compassionate and open and daring way. Sharing it together was healing. Realising that this is an unresolved issue not only individually or even nationally, but that it actually is an issue that we in the Western world all share, divides the weight of the matter on all our shoulders; to look at it in the light of day is a relief and it gives hope that when dealt with together, anything can heal.

These experiences brought home to us the great potential and therefore importance of working with national patterns. We decided to go a step deeper by adopting a more systematic approach and applying the same principles underlying individual- and group-work also on the collective level.

Assagioli's Psychosynthesis of a Nation

Quite late in our own process, ten years after we started our inquiry into Jewishness and the nature of the Jewish people, I was invited to Firenze, into the archives of Roberto Assagioli. There I discovered his work of National Psychosynthesis and, most importantly, his extensive work on the Psychosynthesis of the Jewish people.

To my surprise I saw that what we in Hechal had been doing for a decade was actually the application and further development of the rough outline he had written seventy years earlier.

I include here some excerpts from the Assagioli archive, taken from loose and mostly undated snippets, to give you a taste of his original writing. All of the quotes in this book, except for one at the very end, are taken from the section of the archive called *Studio Archive,* boxes 67 through 71. These boxes contain research material and personal notes pertaining to National Psychosynthesis. I want to express my love and appreciation for Roberto Assagioli and for his selfless, tireless work on behalf of humanity.

"Nations, as individuals, have a 'body' which consists of their material means of expression; that is to say, native soil, geographical position and material assets. In addition each nation has an emotional life consisting of feelings and the modes of reaction prevalent among its citizens, as well as its own 'mentality'. All this constitutes a 'personality', possessing well-defined and recognizable psychological characteristics. We may even go further and say that every nation has a soul."

"The study of national entities as psychological beings brings to light that the greatest part of a nation's psychological life corresponds to that in the individual which takes place at unconscious levels. This life is mainly instinctive, irrational, emotional, imaginative and suggestible, often dominated by elements of the collective unconscious, e.g., ancestral images (such as tradition and myths). It is easy to recognise these characteristics of psychological life in crowds and, to a large extent, in the public at large."

"Every people, from the smallest to the largest, has a job to do, a contribution to make, as everyone has them in the family and in society, we can say that the set of nations is similar to a large orchestra in which each instrument has its own function, so in the concert of nations each has its part to 'play' in the great human symphony."

"Only in this way can each Nation develop and demonstrate the clear vision, the understanding, the goodwill and the generosity which are necessary to make possible and to cooperate towards *international* Psychosynthesis – the wielding of all human units and groups into *one* living world organism."

Collective Transformation:
Meditation 1 – The National Field

*****

Imagine yourself looking at planet Earth from outer space. Visualise Earth surrounded by an orb, an aura, which contains all the emotional and mental activities on the planet.

Notice the different continents, and on each continent the different nations, each with their specific physical, emotional and mental characteristics.

Zoom in now on one nation. Take a moment to get a sense of this nation as a living entity. Notice its location and its surroundings. See if you can discern any emotional and mental patterns. Notice any interaction with surrounding nations.

Bless this nation, and zoom out to bless the planet as a whole, and open your eyes.

*****

How to Work with a National Field

Combining Assagioli's conceptual framework with our experiential work we can summarise that the phases of national psychosynthesis are the same as for individuals and groups: whether it is a person, a group or a nation, the work always starts with the inquiry into the actual state of the personality. Then the flashlight is turned symbolically upwards, to the higher self or soul, in order to receive inspiration and guidance. The third phase then consists of relating the assessment of the present situation and a vision obtained by the soul of a possible future; thus an Ideal Model is formulated, which serves as a guide towards the next step.

On the personal level, this work is done by the Inner Director; in a group, as we have seen, it is the focaliser who leads this process.

On the national level this work must be done by a group. Assagioli calls those who are able to engage in this work 'the Group of Best Citizens'. They constitute in effect the Conscious Self of the nation. Before we get to know this mysterious group, let us reiterate the protocol, as it will serve us as a map and will keep us oriented during the journey through this chapter:

- Looking inwards: observing the national personality
- Looking upwards: invoking the national soul
- Looking outwards: formulating and implementing a vision for the nation

A tall order, right?

The Group of Best Citizens

So it's the 'group of best citizens' who can do the national work. In Assagioli's words (again from the archive boxes stated above): "The self-aware part of the 'national personality' is represented by the minority of people, and especially by those who think: philosophers, historians, scientists, psychologists, and a few statesmen who seek to awaken and develop the true 'consciousness of the nation', to interpret its past and point the way to its future development. But this minority is still, more often than not, at the stage of investigation and research rather than that of sure solutions. Its members are often in disagreement and have contrasting opinions."

Those members of the group of best citizens are individuals, mostly not in cooperation with each other, and may even be, as Assagioli wrote, in conflict with one another.

What is the next needed step for this 'group of best citizens'? I can identify three aspects: one on the level of the individual and two pertaining to group work. The individual member of such a group would profitably go through the process described in the first chapter. In Assagioli's words: "The basic qualification, of which all others are the outcome, is the attainment by the individual of a certain degree of spiritual Psychosynthesis. The man or woman must be to some extent under the influence, the direction and the inspiration of his or her Soul."

Assagioli explains that a person under the guidance of their soul is able to constructively deal with their individual problems, which in turn makes them capable "to vision, understand and help to solve in a similar way all group problems, and particularly those of the national entity, which are much of the same nature, only on a larger scale."

When such trained people also learn to work together as a coherent group, we immediately have much better conditions and a much greater potential. There is a synergy effect. The greater the maturity of the group members and the coherence of the group, the deeper the group can dare to penetrate the uncharted territory of a collective psyche.

The third aspect of improvement is the enlargement of the scope of such a group of best citizens. A certain degree of diversity is needed in the group in order to discern national patterns: how can we recognise our own narrow identifications, which limit our vision of the whole? It is difficult enough to rise above our personal identifications, but it is so much harder to rise above our national conditioning. Think about the fact that we inhale our national identification before we develop our own conscious identity; it is like a conditioning screen we don't even realise is there. We are like fish who will never realise that they swim in water until they are suddenly faced with a different living environment.

We only become aware of our national conditioning if we have people representing different backgrounds in our group; the conditioning of their background is rubbing against ours – in fact, it is this friction which makes us aware of it. When a group can constructively hold such a field of friction, the group members are enabled to look at this phenomenon together, slowly and gradually freeing themselves from it. Only to the degree that we are free, capable of disidentification, from this conditioning screen or fog can we see the wider picture and later the soul potential.

Therefore, in an ideal group of best citizens, there would be people with a certain degree of spiritual Psychosynthesis, from different backgrounds, who are sufficiently able to disidentify from their own national identity – which actually means that they would be more identified with humanity than with their own nation.

Seventy years ago, Assagioli was quite alone with this work; he found no coworkers. Today, more and more citizens in all nations become more self-aware and therefore enter the ranks of the group of 'best citizens', taking responsibility on the national level. Greatly helped by the Internet, the growing members of this self-aware group have today the option to cooperate with each other. This is a new development on our planet. It's a next step on the way of building a critical mass of self-awareness on the national and inter-national level. When the Conscious Self of a nation eventually assumes leadership or at least a guiding role, then the nation will be soul-guided; it will be in process of its spiritual Psychosynthesis, and therefore will be a constructive force among its neighbours and within humanity.

It's this national Conscious Self which can become aware for the first time of the thoughtforms, or mental patterns, that underlie the national entity's life. To look these subtle yet very powerful conditioning factors knowingly in the eye marks the difference between reacting to circumstances like a victim and responding to a situation consciously and constructively.

We may be able to fulfil only partially at the moment these lofty requirements for national work, but we can stretch ourselves in this direction; by experimenting with it through the *doing-as-if* attitude (which we have employed earlier in our personal transformation process), we may at least lay the foundation for later work, charting out a first map. And by imagining an ideal group of best citizens, we create a subtle blueprint for it, a seed for the future.

Collective Transformation:
Meditation 2 – Ideal Group of Best Citizens

*****

Imagine yourself being invited to be part of a group of best citizens of a nation. Imagine entering a beautiful building, and being led to a quiet and spacious room, with a very special atmosphere. In it are seated, perhaps in a circle or half-circle, various people, obviously all members of that nation, but from different backgrounds. Take a look at their faces. They have a rather refined expression, each radiating a degree of wisdom and integrity. It is easy to feel that they love their nation but also are capable to fearlessly and honestly look at its shortcomings. Their motives are pure. Each brings a rich background into the group, a unique angle of their nationality.

Imagine among them different professions – psychologists, historians, sociologists, artists, human rights activists, mothers, religious and spiritual leaders, etc. Take a moment to sense this rich array of national potential.

Now imagine the door opening and a whole group of people entering, women and men, from other countries and continents. Visualise them taking their seats in the shared special space. They have different outwards appearances, yet the same wisdom shines through their faces.

Savour this moment of sitting in the presence of this team, in the rich diversity present in the room, and the maturity of these people who are obviously able to rise above their racial, cultural and religious backgrounds and whose sense of belonging is firmly anchored in the oneness of humanity. True unity in diversity. Sense the potential of both breadth of vision and consecration of heart of such an ideal team of researchers.

A relaxed and yet focused silence settles in the room as this group of best citizens close their eyes, to reflect on the personality of the nation and invoke the national soul.

Take a moment for this to happen. With a blessing for the nation open your eyes.

*****

Towards a Scientific Attitude

A 'group of best citizens', at this point, is basically a research group. However, here we face a few obstacles, with which we have grappled in Hechal. Assagioli has also, from the perspective just after the Second World War, given careful thought on the setting of the right attitude when approaching work with a national collective.

One central issue which is encountered very quickly in this work is the very human tendency of judgementalism. How can we counteract this human reflex? By making the constant effort to balance our inquiring mind with an inclusive heart. Assagioli describes it thus: "In all this work it is essential – in order to avoid harmful mistakes – to keep free from personal and collective bias, emotions and passions. This, after all, means to use and maintain the true scientific attitude necessary in all research work, and known as necessary in all responsible action. But as it is comparatively easy to assume this attitude while observing and/or experimenting with materials, substances, it is most difficult when examining the qualities and the faults of one's nation …"

Assagioli advised not to directly attack a fault, but to use the method of eliminating it through the active cultivation of its opposite.

This takes great discipline and, if adhered to, safeguards the group from unnecessary loops of attack and defence.

It is amazing to see how national work touches all of us below the belt, so to speak, in our unconscious and vulnerable places. Such delicacy, such maturity of heart and soul is needed to tread respectfully on this fragile and explosive ground. That's why national work necessitates a balance and synthesis of truth and love, of mind and heart. Only from a space of love can truth be perceived. Only in a space of love can truth be heard. The effort towards truth must always be reciprocated by an equal effort of love. The more we love, the more will our truth be non-judgmental and therefore non-offensive.

The other noteworthy lesson we learnt could best be called *humility*. As stated, a group of best citizens is a research group; so our work needs to become a scientific laboratory. However, while in a scientific setup there are clear distinctions between the human observer, the method of observation, the subject of observation and the tools of observation, in our case there are no such clear conditions. We ourselves are the observing scientist, the recording and measuring device and part of the subject under observation. It is through our own thoughts and feelings that we observe the national entity, of which we ourselves are a part. There is no such thing as stable lab conditions in this research. While this sounds rather unscientific, we can take solace from the fact that even in the natural sciences there is now an understanding and a wrestling with the fact that stable, controlled and isolated lab conditions simply do not exist.

The fact that all is related doesn't stop in the lab. So, also in science there is a shift happening from separation consciousness to relation consciousness. This new development in science includes taking into account the influence of the observer and the act of observation on the object of observation.

In our research of a collective entity, at this state of development, we must take our own thoughts and feelings as empirical evidence, as specific manifestations of the phenomenon under observation. This is how we need to address them.

Each time one links into a collective field, it is a different experience. Much depends on the state in which we ourselves as the observer enter the research session. And much depends on what is going on at that specific moment in time in the national collective itself, especially if the session is conducted within its local confines. There are factors playing, of which at this point in the pioneering work we are not even aware, much less able to take into account and measure.

With this state of affairs, humility indeed behoves us. And this humility leaves us free – free to approach the subject afresh each time. Each research session brings more facets and details, and brings us towards a higher truth, a higher point of synthesis.

As always, our impressions are interpreted according to our background. That is why it is so important to engage in this process as a group, together with people from different backgrounds, so our national and cultural biases can rub against each other, and the rub can help us to identify them and then disidentify enough from them to see a more inclusive truth, a more complete point of view.

From this humble, soft place, all contributions are welcomed and respected and valued. We all hold a puzzle piece of the national reality and we need one another to see a fuller picture.

At the same time, it is well to strive to be as scientific as possible and to create the most stable lab conditions that we can.

The first and easiest aspect of our lab is the physical outer environment. The physical meeting space should be as free as possible of clutter, noise and any disharmonious influences. In this way we establish a sacred space. The wider atmosphere also has a notable effect on this delicate work. For example, in times of great political tension and fresh violence in Jerusalem we found it more difficult to engage in this work. It needs a certain inner focus and dedication which is difficult to hold steady in a collective field in turmoil.

But for the most part, our lab is our group field; our recording and measuring devices are our personal sensors, feelings, and thoughts. So great care should be given to calibrate ourselves.

Through a process of personal and group alignment, the highest possible quality of attunement and coherence is created. Gradually we establish a telepathic, coherent group field. The more we practice it, the more the field becomes coherent and the more our method of meditative inquiry becomes refined.

In summary I want to reiterate that our efforts are *towards* a scientific attitude. Spiritual research and scientific research still have a stretch to go before this chasm will be bridged.

The last thing to do before starting the actual meditative inquiry is to consecrate our minds and hearts, much like a doctor or therapist ought to do before a treatment session. We dedicate ourselves to act as the Conscious Self of the nation, and strive to align our consciousness with its soul.

Looking Inwards – Observing the National Personality

The following broad-stroked outline is a synthesis garnered from our years of experiential work in Hechal and Assagioli's conceptual framework. It uses the Jewish people here and there as an example, but is applicable to any nation.

We start our observation on the physical level, and then move on to the emotional and mental components.

The Physical Field of a Nation

To inquire into the physical aspect of a nation is relatively easy, because it's based on measurable facts; we can see the physical presence of a nation on the map, with its characteristics, liabilities and resources, with its rural areas and cities and the roads connecting them. Each member of the nation is a cell in the nation, much like the cells in a human body.

And here we encounter an intriguing point. When observing a national entity we cannot fail to notice the fact that, just as the cells of the human body are constantly being replaced by new ones, so the human beings which are part of the collective at any one time are being constantly replaced.

It was a huge eye-opener for me when I suddenly realised that there was a difference between the national psyche and the human beings who embody it at any one time.

This brings us to the question of reincarnation. While it is not necessary to endorse the belief in reincarnation in order to engage in collective work, it is helpful to accept it as a working hypothesis. This is what I and my group and also Assagioli did. In this hypothesis, all life is one: we all come from one source and journey together through many incarnations within the evolutionary flow, according to various laws and cycles; at the end of this journey we will all have found our way back home to our common source. According to this theory all humans incarnate periodically in different races, cultures, and religions.

This theory of reincarnation gives us a greater context for the phenomenon under observation. In our case that meant the inspiring idea that most of us may have had Jewish and non-Jewish incarnations. This idea had a soothing effect in that it blurred the sharp separation line between Jews and non-Jews – portraying it as something temporary rather than being an ingrained and unchangeable fact.

The Emotional Field of a Nation

To observe the emotional aspect of a collective is more difficult and evasive, just as it is in the case of an individual human being. We don't see an emotional field with our eyes, and moreover it is more diversified and dynamic than the physical. The emotional field of a nation contains all its lines of connection – the family ties, the communities, the business interactions, the religious cohesiveness, etc. Likewise contained within it are all the nation's emotional reactions over the centuries and millennia of its existence: there are the more superficial, short-lived feelings and momentary moods and fluctuations, and there are the emotional patterns and characteristics which have formed over a long period of time.

Each experience in the collective life elicits an emotional reaction. When an experience is repeated often, the emotional reaction to it becomes a tendency, built into the system as a character trait. Likewise, a very strong experience can, even if happening only once, have such a strong impact that it will forever be imprinted in the national psyche.

In regard to the Jewish people, we may turn our thoughts to the event at Mount Sinai, where God made a pact with the Jewish people, as a profound imprint on the collective. And we may think of the persecutions the Jewish people have suffered over millennia, having shaped a powerful defence mechanism in the Jewish psyche.

What profound healing is needed to undo this?

The Mental Field of a Nation

In the same way that the emotional field generates feelings, the mental field generates and contains our thoughts. The same way as habitual emotions turn into emotional tendencies over time, repeated thoughts turn into mental constructs – so-called *thoughtforms* – which filter our experience.

We have briefly touched upon thoughtforms when we explored the personal mental field. Here is a little more on how thoughtforms come about and how they function: our mind reacts to each experience we have, tries to give meaning to it, interprets it; when an experience is especially strong or significant, our interpretation of it develops into a belief and a concept; when we keep thinking about it, it becomes a mental construct.

Think of this construct as an object, made of mental matter. The more we think about it the more solid and powerful it becomes. At a certain critical mass, a thoughtform will express itself on the physical plane. This happens on the individual, group and collective level. On the collective level, for example, when a religious impulse becomes strong enough, a temple will eventually be built. This is the manifestation of our underlying premise of 'energy follows thought'.

As is an individual mind so also a collective mind is a creative agent. Wherever we direct the power of our thought, there we create. So a collective mind creates collective thoughtforms. The collective mind contains the thoughts, ideas and beliefs around which the collective has been formed. Generations of thinkers add to it – the big thinkers add brilliance and breadth, and the small thinkers add distortions and density.

All human beings are born into collective thoughtforms and are conditioned by them before they have a chance to choose. As we incarnate and then reincarnate, we are exposed to different thoughtforms and participate in their generation and perpetuation.

Take a moment …

*****

Contemplate the following fact: we as souls change roles, but the thoughtforms we create remain and condition the following generations, and may condition us in our own future incarnation.

*****

In the process of repetition and unavoidable distortion, thoughtforms become crystallised and hardened. Such crystallised thinking can trap an individual and whole nations in very narrow perceptions about reality. This can lead to fundamentalism, separativeness and isolation. It is actually an overdose of mental constructs. Strong minds tend to build strong mental constructs. Minds are separate by definition. They analyse, which means they take apart. They isolate.

When we are totally identified with our mind, we are controlled by it and by the thoughtforms it builds – both individually and collectively. We build prisons for ourselves, and we can only free ourselves from our self-built confinements by disidentifying from them through identifying with something higher or bigger. For the individual this may mean to open their heart to someone else, or to become soul-conscious; for a nation this means to see itself as part of a bigger whole, part of the family of humanity.

Therefore, freedom has a lot to do with disidentifying from the creation of our minds.

Once we have this in place – that we are creative beings, that we create thoughtforms, that we tend to get trapped in our own creations and that we can through a process of self-reflection free ourselves from our identification with these thoughtforms – then we have a choice, then we have freedom, on the individual and national level.

This is of course a central theme for all of humanity, but perhaps especially pertinent for the Jewish people, because of their exceptionally brilliant mind. In Hechal's meditative inquiries we often perceived the Jewish mind as a diamond. It seems to have 360 degrees of facets and angles of endless creativity. There is a truly wide spectrum of capabilities. And at the same time this diamond is 'a hard nut'. It's difficult to disidentify from it.

After this short overview of the various components of the national entity, we will now open our finer antennae to meditatively probe into them. The following is a general first view. This exercise seems very simple, but it requires a shift in our mode of perception. We must temporarily suspend the control of our concrete mind – to create a space of stillness in our mind into which more subtle impressions can be received. Sometimes it takes a while for such impressions to be registered, because we are not familiar with them. They may come in the form of images, feelings, memories, even bodily sensations. With continued use, we learn to listen to these less used antennae and to refine them. With experience, as our focus gradually sharpens and deepens, our inquiry can become more specific.

Collective Transformation:
Meditation 3 – Observation of the National Personality

*****

Visualise yourself in the beautiful building together with the Ideal Group of Best Citizens, dedicated to represent the Conscious Self of the nation. As part of this group, draw a line upwards to the soul of the nation. Endeavour to keep the alignment with the national soul throughout the following observation.

Direct your attention now to the physical expression of the nation – its location on the planet, its shape, its neighbours; the physical bodies of its citizens, their houses, villages, cities.

Envision the connections between them – family ties; communities; business connections; religious ties. Note also the divisions between various factions.

Get an overall sense of the vitality of this collective organism.

Take a moment to reflect on it.

Imagine now before your mind's eye the nation as a subtle field, which contains all its emotional dynamics. Reflect on the prevalent emotional characteristics of the nation. Bring to mind significant experiences in the collective life, and their emotional responses. What is the general emotional atmosphere of this nation?

Focus now on the thought life of the nation.

What characterises this collective mind? Is it possible to identify the main thoughtforms around which the nation is built? What is the underlying belief system of the nation?

Take a moment to get a felt sense of the national mental world.

Now release the observation. Visualise a blessing from the national soul passing through the mental, emotional and physical fields of the nation and open your eyes.

*****

Looking Upwards – Invoking the National Soul

We reach now to the second phase in the work of the National Psychosynthesis: the invocation of the national soul.

Here we are treading on sacred – and quite unknown – ground.

Assagioli said that "the soul of a nation manifests itself in three ways: through great individuals, isolated or in small groups; through collective manifestations; and through the steady influence of its best citizens."

No one person can fully represent the soul of a nation. But a great leader, a genius, a venerable religious figure, a social activist, an inspiring artist, all these express an aspect of the national soul.

We can get a glimpse of the national soul at exceptional moments and significant events in the life of a nation. We can train ourselves to recognise the manifestations of it by looking at its history and present circumstances. It can give us indications as to its specific mission. One question which can guide us to discern the national soul is: how can this nation contribute to the human family?

In times of national crisis the national soul's wisdom can be drawn forth by individuals and groups, causing sometimes unimagined humanitarian action in response to dire needs.

The soul of a nation holds the nation's innermost purpose and destiny, and its highest aspirations. It is a source of inspiration and guidance at any one junction on the nation's path. It is the collective super-conscious or higher wisdom, with which we, individuals and groups, can and eventually should be in regular communion.

Assagioli pointed out that in the future regular rituals or ceremonies to invoke the soul of a nation will be held, especially before important national meetings and big decisions.

This is to be done by people who have developed the aptitude to be in direct contact with the higher wisdom of the nation.

This is the most delicate and sacred part of the work with a national entity. The sensing and invoking of a national soul requires a very clear and free mind and a consecrated heart. We must approach it with humility and reverence.

Let us do this now in our imagination in the following exercise.

Collective Transformation:
Meditation 4 – Invocation of the National Soul

*****

See yourself among the group of best citizens, in the special place of gathering. Dedicate yourself to be a representative of the Conscious Self of the nation and consecrate your heart and mind in preparation for meeting the soul of the nation.

As part of the group of best citizens, open yourself to the highest aspect of the nation, its soul and its purpose. Take a moment to sit in silent receptivity. Note any impressions, about the true nature of the nation, its purpose and function in the larger whole of humanity and any next steps.

Take a moment to let these impressions take form in your brain consciousness, as words.

Now visualise the light of the national soul radiate downwards into the national mind. See it strengthen all thoughtforms which resonate with its essence. And let it disperse all thoughtforms which are no longer needed, those which are fear-based, and hold the nation in the past. See the national mind clear and strong, an instrument for the common good.

Now visualise the love of the national soul radiate into the national emotions.

See it strengthen all feelings that are in resonance with this purpose and essence. And visualise any trauma being healed, all fear-based emotions and separations released and dissipated. See the national heart radiating, giving of itself to all.

Now visualise the will and power of the national soul radiate into the physical outer expression of the nation. See those outer forms which resonate with this essence being strengthened. And all those forms, customs, laws, behaviour, which are fear-based and of the past, being released and forgotten. Visualise the nation building the right outer forms which express the inner essence, to the highest good of all its citizens.

Visualise the nation in right relation with the rest of Humanity.

Visualise a blessing from the soul of the nation streaming through the whole national personality out into the world.

*****

Looking Outwards – Formulating a Vision for the Nation

How would an ideal group of best citizens go about formulating a new vision for their nation? After shared silent contemplation, they would listen to each other and compile all their 'findings' about the national personality. They would likewise collect all higher impressions and inspirations received into the group field. From relating the assessment of the present situation to the glimpses of vision towards the future they would then draw up a plan with practical steps. This plan would be held into the light of the nation's soul in consecutive meditations and it would be refined and solidified until it could be shared with the thinkers and leaders of the nation.

Such a plan would be an instance of what Assagioli called an 'Ideal Model' – a vision or image of what could be the nation's achievements as a contribution to humanity. That necessarily would require looking at the nation not only by itself but rather as part of a wider, overall plan for humanity as a whole.

How self-evident and easy it sounds, and how far we still are from it! This profound work requires such a high degree of inner integrity and sustained striving. It is the striving towards a completed point of view concerning the destiny of a nation. As yet, the entire General Assembly of the United Nations cannot do this. We can only humbly try.

Formulating a vision for a nation calls for the effort to keep in mind as full a picture as we can of the present situation of a nation, without judging. Furthermore, to remain open to impression from the national soul. This is an ongoing process. Over the years there will develop a solidifying sense of knowing something of the destiny of the nation. The daily national happenings are then interpreted in this light, and underlying trends are recognised. A kind of impersonal love and care for the nation grows.

How wonderful it would be if there existed such a group of best citizens in each nation, which would be consulted on major decisions. To have such delegates at the United Nations – what a world we would have!

Implementing the Vision

Like so many other individuals and transformation groups, at the end of 2012 we in Hechal had felt a distinct shift in the subtle energies on our planet. It seemed the lowest point in the planetary crisis had been reached, and the scales were now subtly shifting towards the light. While the outer happenings of the time continued to worsen, the love and light underlying them became more visible. The transformation work began to be less of an uphill struggle, and this tendency has grown more distinct since.

In line with this development, we felt it was time to move to a different phase in our work as a group. After many years of teaching meditation and self-development, of learning the skills to function as a transformation group, of deep research into the Jewish collective, we felt now ready for a more proactive project.

At that time an international member of our group had a dream in which our group ran a radio broadcast from Jerusalem, each group member having a specific function. The dream seemed to contain the essential elements for our next step:

Jerusalem is in many ways the capsule containing the quintessence of what the Jewish people are about, including its greatest challenge today: the experiment of a democratic Israel and its relationship with the Arab Palestinians.

Radio – or, more precisely, Internet communication – is the new way of cooperation. Online group work makes it possible to connect over physical distances and over the divide of separation walls and checkpoints.

We decided to reach out to our Arab Palestinian co-workers from our meditation courses and full moon meetings, and hold regular online meditations as a common contribution to right relations in Jerusalem. For a while some of them joined us, but little by little they left. With sadness, we realised that the time for this type of cooperation was not yet ripe. The divide was still too big, too painful. What worked in local, physical meetings, with much personal heart-sharing, didn't work online; touching the core of the deep wound existing between Jews and Arabs needs the physical presence of human closeness, with authentic, vulnerable eye contact and the warmth of real physical hugs.

Of course, Jerusalem as the archetypal City of Peace has significance not only for the local population but symbolically for the whole world. To expand into a larger than local context was also a growing need in our group. We felt that for our work to 'breathe properly' it needed to be more connected to the world at large. To interact with others from around the world felt like an energetic lifeline. We needed what Assagioli called 'spiritual airways': "It is urgent to establish spiritual airways between nations, institutions, movements and across the continents – let us give to this work comparatively at least as much energy, determination, service, time, efforts as those which are given to establish airplane communications throughout the world." (This inspiring phrase has been found on a little scrap paper in the archive and is dated 20.9.1937. Out of it has emerged the recent initiative of the Psychosynthesis community to hold an annual International Psychosynthesis Day on that day, September 20.)

We built a core team of eight people, made up of members of the Hechal group and some international co-workers. We decided to hold weekly online meetings for meditation and discussion about right relations in Jerusalem.

So our group consists of local Jewish Jerusalemites and international spiritual co-workers from a Christian background.

It is not the whole spectrum one would wish for in an ideal group of best citizens, but it is a band of co-workers of high quality. It is part of a pioneering work, a stretch of consciousness in which people from different countries work as a group, learning to go beyond their identification with their specific background and to identify with the larger whole of the *One Humanity*: in such initiatives, such stretches of consciousness, using the power of our minds and the consecration of our hearts for the planetary common good, we practice becoming a unified human family. This 'group of best world citizens' is the new phenomenon on our planet, the emerging Conscious Self of humanity.

Our Jerusalem Meditation work in its different stages reflects the steps outlined in this book: We set out beginning with ourselves, sharing the daily grievances of life in Jerusalem, especially in times of heightened conflict and violence, and also realising that the same difficulties are happening all over the world. We took these grievances with us into meditation. We learnt to contain them in our group field and by this loving containment much transmuting and healing could take place in each of us, thereby contributing to the transmuting of the collective patterns pertaining to Jerusalem.

We immersed ourselves into the deeper nature of Jerusalem – its origins, its significance for the three Abrahamic religions and therefore for the whole Western and Muslim world. We worked extensively with the pain of division within the city. And gradually we began shifting our attention from the illness to the cure. The cure for separativeness can only come through the human heart, through the simple and yet so very difficult understanding that we are all human beings, that it is about the human condition rather than about this religion or that, this nation or that.

We started to look out for signs of the New Jerusalem among the happenings of the time. We now share each week before our meditation a few local and sometimes global good news pertaining to the shift from separation consciousness to relation consciousness, empowering these signs of the new world by holding them in our group consciousness.

Our regular online meditation meetings are like a rhythmical administering of a medicine. With our meditation outline evolving over the years, our 'formula' is constantly being refined, and our 'medical team' becomes more professional, learning new skills all the time.

The cure, as we said, is love.

Relation consciousness.

The New Jerusalem is simply the open human heart. There, separativeness is transcended into oneness. Love thy neighbour as thyself. But it takes more than the romantic sentiment we often associate with this phrase; it implies quite the opposite, in fact. This work demands a rigorous discipline: on the one hand not to be afraid to feel the pain of what is happening in Jerusalem every day, keeping a vulnerable, loving heart; and on the other, to be quite above these daily happenings, detached, holding the much wider picture, the intended vision of a Jerusalem of right relations among all inhabitants.

That requires standing with full intention and with full strength and presence. It is an act of will. It involves taking a firm stand for right relations, for peace. It means to affirm the common good within our thoughts, feelings and actions. It is a daily practice of cultivating in ourselves both will and love. When we sustain that, the two are forged into a synthesis, which we call *The Will to Love*.

Take a moment …

*****

Contemplate this phrase: 'The Will to Love'. It connotes in actuality the decision to be a peace-commanding presence. Remain a moment longer with trying on the decision to be a peace-commanding presence. Sense the potency of it.

*****

This is the 'medicine' we administer to the field of Jerusalem every week. Our Jerusalem online work is open once a month, at the new moon, to participants from all around the globe, and everyone is welcome.

Similar global initiatives are springing up everywhere. The Will to Love, the synthesis of the first ray of will and power and the second ray of love and wisdom, is needed everywhere. It is *Love* which heals and unites our world, and it is *Will* which makes sure it gets done.

When we start caring for our world at large, we become fired by a higher cause, purpose and will than our own. A stronger will wakes up in us and starts to work through us. We say a resounding *Yes!*

Yes, I will stand for the common good.

People everywhere standing in the Will to Love, becoming a peace-commanding presence – this is the new bottom line. It is this inner attitude or alignment which, underneath the disintegrating forms of our old world, becomes gradually visible. We are on the way to becoming awakened, empowered human beings. For those who have eyes to see, the Conscious Self of humanity is in process of taking the reins in hand.

Much remains to be explored about cooperation on the level of groups. And we are still just at the beginning of learning to work with collective patterns, invoking a national soul and weaving 'spiritual airways'. I hope this book will stimulate further research and cooperation between groups.

Rabbi Abraham Isaac Kook, the first Chief Rabbi of Israel, sums up the whole process we have been covering in this book in this beautiful passage:

"There is the person who sings the song of his own soul. Within his own soul he finds all that he needs. Then there is the person who sings the song of his nation, who goes beyond the narrow circle of his own soul and lovingly embraces the collectivity of his people. And then there is the person whose soul expands until it goes beyond the limits of his people, singing the song of mankind, his soul growing and expanding with the collective pride of mankind and the glory of the Divine image in man, drawing the broad strokes of his ideas from this source of life.

But there is also the one who goes even beyond this, until he becomes one with the entire cosmos, with all of its creatures, with all the worlds, and with all of them he sings a song."

The work of creating coherent fields and right relationships goes beyond nations and beyond even the human kingdom. To complete Rabbi Kook's song, we also need to sing with the nature kingdom and with the higher worlds.

But that is for another book.

We conclude our Jerusalem Meditation with the *Mantram of Unification*, by Alice Bailey, which Assagioli also used daily. It is a fitting ending for this book, for all our Relations.

Collective Transformation:
Meditation 5 – Mantram of Unification

*****

The souls of all are one and I am one with them.
I seek to love, not hate:
I seek to serve and not exact due service.
I seek to heal, not hurt.
Let pain bring due reward of light and love.
Let the soul control the outer form
and life and all events,
and bring to light the love which underlies
the happenings of the time.
Let vision come and insight;
let the future stand revealed.
Let inner union demonstrate
and outer cleavages be gone.
Let love prevail.
Let all people love.

*****